Pulled Thread Embroidery

Pulled Thread Embroidery

Moyra McNeill

Taplinger Publishing Company | New York

First published in the United States in 1972 by
TAPLINGER PUBLISHING COMPANY
New York, New York

Library of Congress Catalog Card Number: 70-185624

ISBN 0-8008-6562-6

Acknowledgements

I am sincerely grateful to the following:

the Whitworth Art Gallery, University of Manchester, the Liverpool City Museums, Gawthorpe Hall, the Embroiderers Guild, and the Victoria and Albert Museum, who have all been most helpful in allowing their collections to be studied;

the Royal School of Needlework and in particular the members of the class in Autumn 1969 for allowing their work to be photographed;

Miss M Forbes, Mrs. Alison Barrell and students of the Textile Group of Beckenham and Penge Adult Education Centre for their generous help and for allowing their work to be borrowed and photographed;

Miss Crawshaw and girls of Great Yarmouth Technical High School;

all those people who contributed information and ideas.

I would also like to thank the many people who most kindly lent their work to be photographed but which for technical reasons it was not possible to include in this book.

CONTENTS

WHAT IS PULLED THREAD?

Many people are deterred from trying some forms of embroidery simply because their names imply that they are complicated and difficult to learn. There is also a certain mystique about methods like pulled work because some teachers in the past have bounded the technique with rules and strictures which in turn have suggested difficulties that do not exist. It is true that there are one or two extremely complicated stitches which do require concentration, but the aim of this book is to prove how much can be achieved with a basically simple technique, although for those people who wish to go further the challenge of more complex ideas is also presented.

Pulled work and drawn fabric are synonymous, but as drawn fabric can so easily be confused with drawn thread work, pulled thread seems the clearer title. In pulled thread work the threads of the ground material are compressed by pulling stitches tightly, thus forming patterns of holes, and in drawn thread work threads are actually removed from the ground material, usually before any stitching is begun; so although the finished effects of the two methods are vaguely similar the methods are quite different in execution.

Pulled work is also a part of 'linen embroidery', which is a term used by Women's Institutes for a variety of techniques worked on linen.

The use of stitch tension is the main principle that must be understood, as this is the basis of all pulled work. The simplest way to begin is to work a row of satin stitch over four threads, first slackly and then pulling as tightly as possible on the thread. The contrast of effect will be quite obvious. By using this contrast of tension throughout a range of stitches, both rich and lacy textures will be produced, each forming a foil for the other and thus being shown to their best advantage.

An explanation of texture is relevant here: texture is not an abstract term but applies to the surface that is presented to the eye and touch; texture surrounds us in everyday life in walls, floors, clothing, furniture, pavements, roads, grass and plants, and these present surfaces that can be read as smooth, rough, even, shiny, ribbed and so on. If our environment is made up of only one texture it soon becomes boring – for example, rows of brick houses in repetitive streets – but by contrasting brick with trees, grass and paved areas a textural contrast is achieved which is more pleasant simply because it is more varied, and the same general principle applies to the use of texture in much craft work.

A misconception is that pulled work can only be white or beige; this is not true as colour can be used, but after experiment the author has come to the conclusion that pulled work is essentially a monochrome method, as the tightly tensioned stitches are ugly in themselves and it is only when they are completely integrated with the ground material, producing patterns of holes, that they look attractive. Therefore it is quite possible to use rich and bright colours with matching threads, and these can immediately give a more modern effect to a method which has a staid and frumpish image; white can be used effectively on any pale colour as the tone contrast is insufficient to allow any tensioned stitches to show.

Another misconception is that pulled work is essentially very fine and trying to the eyes; while fine work is beautiful, equally effective work can be produced on surprisingly coarse materials and will take a great deal less time.

Nowadays in shops it is possible to see fabrics that have been woven by machine with a texture closely resembling counted thread embroidery. By embroidering all over material repetitively it is possible to produce a very similar effect, which is quite pointless as this by-the-yard look nullifies craftsmanship. The whole point of hand crafts is that they should show individuality and thoughtfulness in design.

There are always people who are naturally attracted by any work on the counted thread, but with the modern, less inhibited approach many other needlewomen may now find this kind of embroidery within their interest and scope.

MATERIALS AND THREADS

Today we have a vast selection of materials and threads to choose from, but as many of the traditional materials and threads go out of production, we are put on our mettle to select the right material for the method. The availability of materials varies from month to month, so that to suggest any one material by name would appear to be pointless, and therefore this chapter will deal with materials in general terms.

For pulled work the fabric must be evenly woven, that is, having the same number of threads per inch or centimetre in warp and weft, and be slightly open in weave, because too close a weave will only cause the material to pucker when pulled stitches are worked on it. The more open the weave the lacier will be the effect, but the most openly woven fabrics have the drawback that they are not suitable for articles to be regularly laundered as the threads can be easily displaced.

For a beginner the best idea would be to write to or visit a reputable supplier of embroidery materials and ask for samples of suitable materials from which a selection can be made, choosing one whose threads can be seen comfortably without strain. Today there is a reasonable range of both white and coloured even-weave linens and cottons, from fairly fine to quite coarse; one point to watch is that coloured fabrics

13

have not been vat-dyed, as this can mean that the colour has not fully penetrated the yarn and white flecks show when threads are pulled aside with stitchery.

Once some experience has been gained, materials can be selected from furnishing or dress fabric counters; curtaining materials of synthetic fibres can often be found with an even weave, of exciting colour and of sufficient width to make table linen; some dress linens can be suitable for pulled work, but synthetics are best worked in a frame so that the maximum tension can be exerted on their frequently springy fibres.

Two cheap materials that are particularly useful are scrim, sold for window cleaning, and dishcloth cotton. Dishcloth cotton has a particularly open weave and is best used when learning, or experimentally.

As a general guide the following may be helpful:

Linen
Even weave available from specialist embroidery suppliers in colours or white (expensive). Scrim for window cleaning; mid-brown but can be bleached or dyed (inexpensive). Dress linens by careful selection.

Cotton
Even weave available from specialist embroidery suppliers in white or colours (reasonably priced). Dishcloth cotton; cream in colour but can be dyed (inexpensive).
White canvas; available from art needlework shops for experimental pulled thread (reasonably priced).

Synthetic fibres
Moygashel dress materials.
Furnishing fabrics in a variety of colours, widths and prices.
Curtaining sheers; wide; some exciting colours.

14

Wool
Woollen fabrics can sometimes be found with even weaves but are often closely woven so that the fibres do not lend themselves to pulled work.

THREADS
Since a twisted linen embroidery thread is no longer available the choice of a thread can be a problem, as it must be strong enough to withstand a considerable strain, and the following is a list of possibilities which will require experiment by the worker to find which suits her purpose:

Clark's extra strong button thread.
Coats' extra strong thread (6).
Buttonhole twist.
Crochet threads from fine (80) to thick (trade names Stalite, Crysette).
Range of colours in *coton à broder* (18) and a variety of sizes in white.
Pearl cotton, from thick (3) through sizes 5, 8, to 12 (finest).
Lace threads.
Fine string.

The following may be used in desperation where no other thread is available, but with the tension required in this method they either break or go fuzzy and should therefore be used in short lengths only:

Anchor linen embroidery thread.
Sylko (40).
Stranded cotton.

By experiment it may be found that an unravelled warp thread of the ground material will be strong enough to embroider with, a solution that saves both time and energy.

To match thread and material, it is possible to dye

threads and material together if the directions for dyes sold in ordinary hardware shops are followed explicitly, or experiments could be made with natural dyes like onion skins. While it is annoying that a prolonged search for materials inevitably precedes any form of imaginative embroidery, it does ensure a lively approach to their selection which may well prevent a stagnation of ideas and in fact lead to new trains of thought and development which would not otherwise have occurred.

STITCHES

On the following pages are given a variety of stitches which, when worked, display a range of textures, beginning with simple forms of counted satin stitch, and growing increasingly more difficult technically. If you are a beginner, work chronologically through the stitches, and when you have finished you will have a sampler showing the texture of each stitch and will also have discovered which stitches are most enjoyable to work and look at.

TECHNICAL HINTS
Needles
Always use tapestry needles for pulled stitches as the blunt point will not split the threads of the fabric.

Framing
So that threads of the ground material may be more easily counted, the fabric may be mounted in either square or circular frames, which may also save having to stretch the embroidery when completed. Keep the material really taut in the frame; this will mean retensioning the material frequently if working on a piece over a length of time.

To begin a thread there are two ways
Either begin by darning in the thread where it will be covered with stitchery, taking a back stitch to secure it, or leave a 3″ (8 cm) end which can be darned into the

back of the stitchery when it is completed. Darn the
ends in immediately, as a forest of ends on the back
can only be a nuisance.

To end
Darn into the back of the stitchery as invisibly as
possible, taking a small back stitch to secure it.

Counting diagonally
Most people find it confusing to count diagonally
across threads, so that if it is necessary to count, for
example, 4 threads diagonally, count across 4, then
down or up 4.

Long jumps across back of work
These are to be avoided where practicable as they may
either snag in laundering or show through on the right
side. If a long jump is unavoidable, darn the thread
under or through a thread of the ground material
about every $\frac{1}{4}''$ (6 mm) on the wrong side.

Turning
When it is necessary to come up in the same hole in
which the previous row finished, take a small stitch
over one thread about three threads away from the
hole to secure it; do not pull tightly.

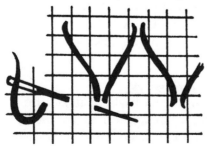

About the photographs in this chapter
The samples have been worked on a bold material and have been slightly enlarged so that each stitch is visible. The effect of the stitchery can be altered considerably by varying the weight and scale of the material; very fine open materials will produce a lace-like effect and more closely woven materials a more restrained texture.

About the diagrams
On the graph paper each line represents a thread of material and each square the space in between the threads. Dotted lines show where the thread lies on the wrong side. Each stitch is shown over a specific number of threads but this may need to be varied depending on the scale of the material in use. Try a little of each stitch on an odd piece of fabric before working it *in situ* to make sure the scale is right.

* indicates that a slack tension should be used, that is, do not pull the thread at all.
** indicates that medium tension should be applied with enough pressure to compress and distort the threads of the ground material.
*** indicates that a really tight tension should be applied, pulling on the thread as hard as possible, and needs very strong thread.

Thickness of thread
As a general rule the thread used for pulled work should be the thickness of a thread from the ground material. Untensioned satin stitch requires a thicker thread.

STITCHES BASED ON SATIN STITCH

A great range of stitches are based on satin stitch worked straight on the thread of the material or diagonally. The stitch may be left loose or pulled tight depending on the effect required. Satin stitch on the counted thread is worked between each thread of the ground material.

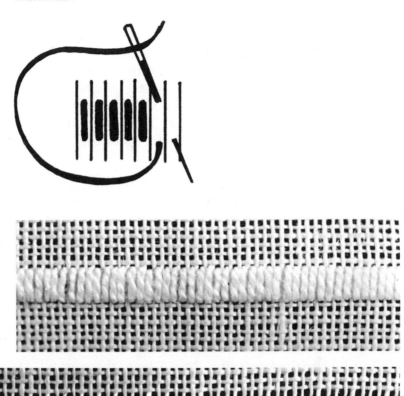

These examples clearly show the effect of tension. The wide stitch was worked over 4 threads slackly * and the narrow one also over 4 threads but tightly ***.

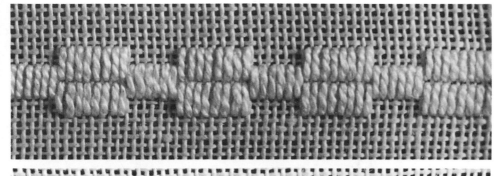

Both these examples were worked in blocks over 4 threads but one * and the other *** with quite different finished results.

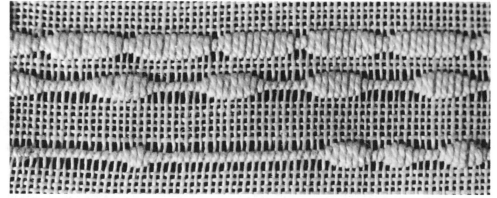

The three lines of stitching here show variations in tension.

Top: 10 * stitches, then 3 *** stitches.
Middle: Alternately 8 * and 8 *** stitches.
Bottom: Stitches worked * or *** at random.

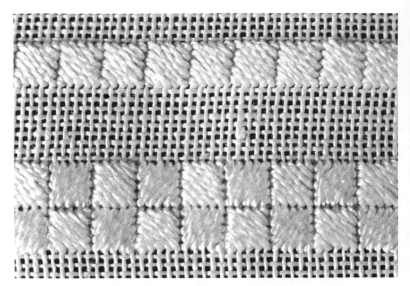

Above are blocks worked diagonally over 1, 2, 3, 4, 5, 4, 3, 2, 1 threads to form a continuous line, and then as a double row slanting in opposing directions *****.

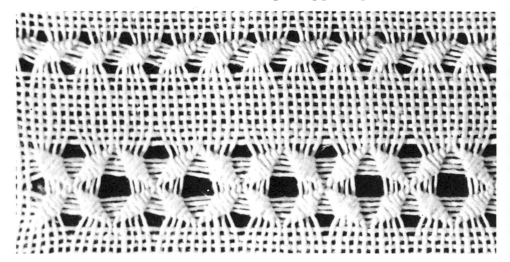

By tightening the tension to ******* quite a different effect is achieved. In order to see the threads clearly work in a frame with the material stretched tautly.

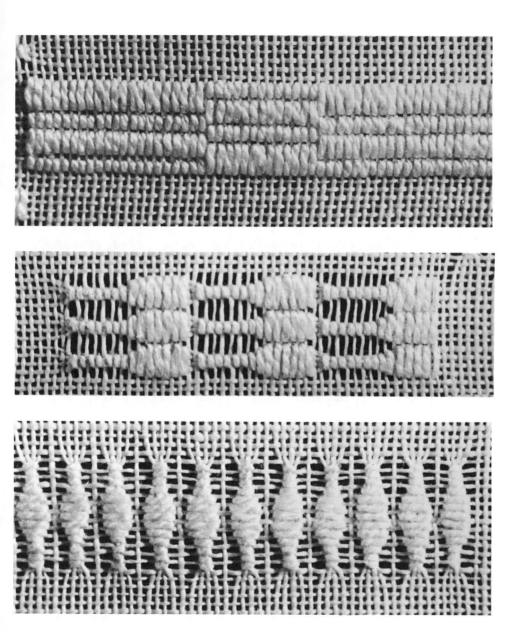

Rows of satin stitching combined to form simple
borders that could be made any width.

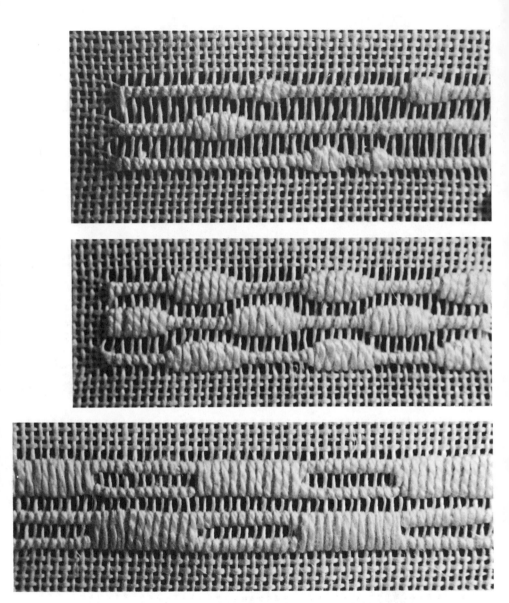

Rows of satin stitching combined to form simple borders that could be made any width.

FILLINGS BASED ON SATIN STITCH

Unless otherwise stated stitches are worked between each thread of the ground material.

Chessboard filling

Blocks of 3 rows of 10 stitches over 3 threads worked in opposing directions; either * or ***.

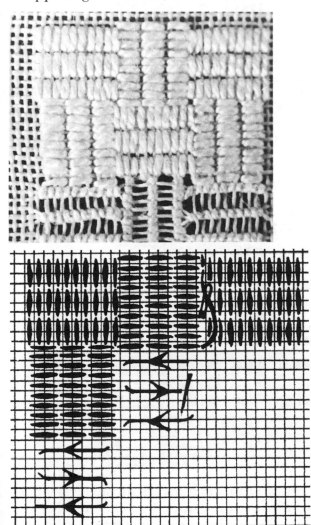

Small chessboard filling

Blocks of 2 rows of 7 stitches over 3 threads, in opposing directions; either * or ***.

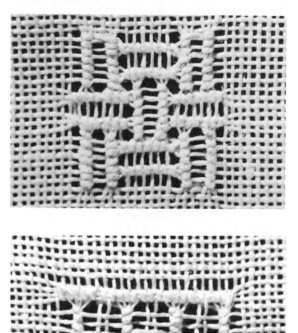

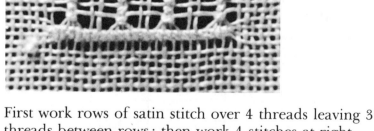

First work rows of satin stitch over 4 threads leaving 3 threads between rows; then work 4 stitches at right angles leaving 2 threads between each (***).

Work blocks of 5 stitches over 4 threads leaving 6
threads in between, overlapping the blocks by 1 thread
(* or ***).

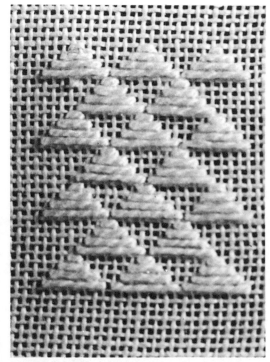

Triangles based on straight stitches over 2, 4, 6, 8
threads, worked in rows diagonally (*).

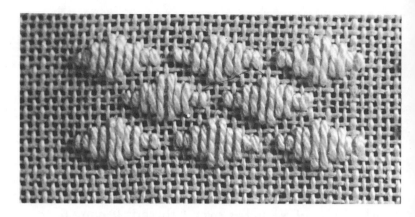

Diamonds formed of 2 stitches over 2, 4, 6, 4, 2
threads, worked in rows leaving 2 threads in between
(*).

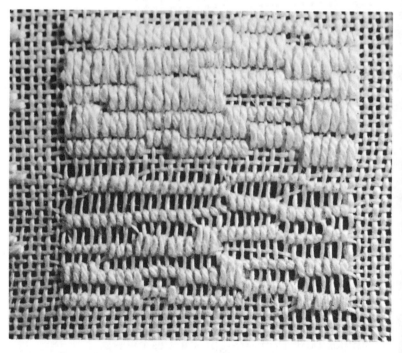

Rows of stitches worked in random widths (* or ***).

Step stitch

Worked diagonally; blocks of 5 stitches over 4 threads at right angles to each other.

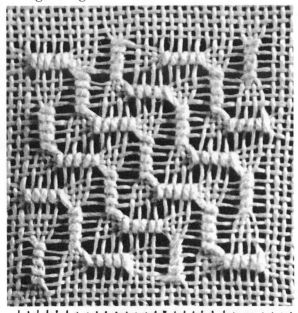

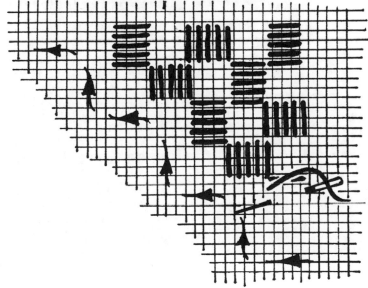

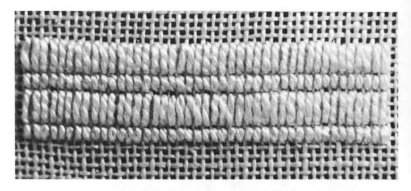

Alternating rows over 4 and 2 threads.

Basket filling is similar to step stitch in movement.

Blocks of 6 stitches over 3 threads are worked at right angles to each other in diagonal rows.

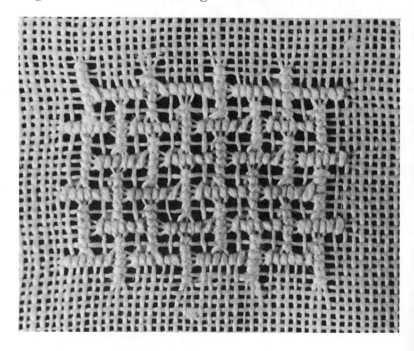

SPACED SATIN STITCH FILLINGS

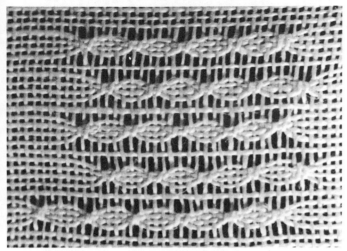

Rows of 2 stitches over 4 threads leaving 5 threads in between; 1 thread left between the rows (**).

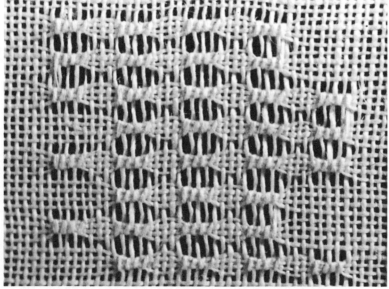

Rows of 4 stitches over 4 threads with 5 threads in between (**).

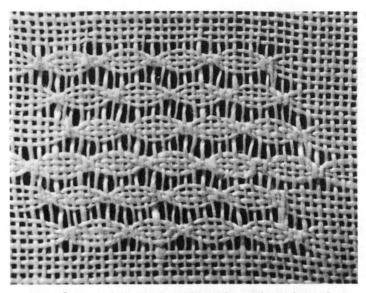

Lines of 2 stitches over 4 threads with 6 threads in between; each line begins 2 threads higher than the previous one (**).

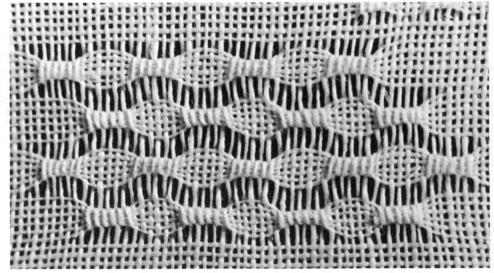

Blocks of 6 stitches over 6 threads with 7 threads in between. Rows bricked (**).

Cobbler filling is not as difficult as it looks. Work 1 stitch over 4 threads, leave 2 threads, 1 stitch over 4 threads, leave 4 threads, and repeat to end of row. Work all rows in one direction first, then repeat the rows at right angles (***).

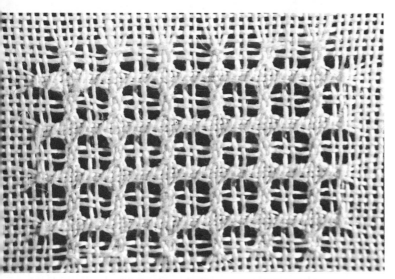

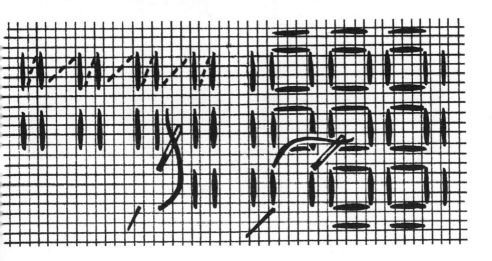

Framed cross filling is worked in the same way as cobbler filling but over a different number of threads, which can be counted from the diagram (✳✳✳).

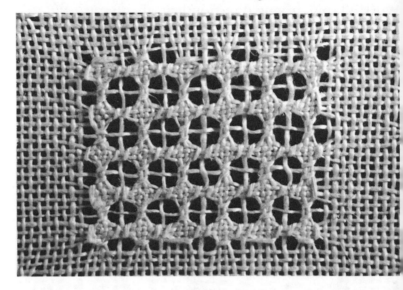

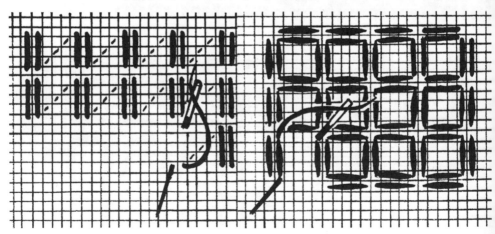

Mock faggot filling

Work 2 stitches over the same 4 threads, leave 4 threads and repeat to form a row. Work all the rows in one direction, then link up by repeating rows at right angles using the same holes.

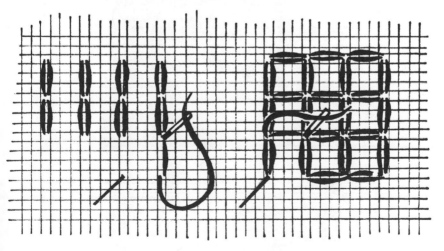

EYELETS

Eyelets are a form of satin stitch, but all the stitches converge on a common centre hole or holes. Bring the needle up on the outer edge and down through the centre for all forms of this stitch because this pulls the centre hole larger. Because of the number of stitches through one hole it is sometimes necessary to use a rather thin thread.

Square eyelet as shown is worked over a square of 8 threads. Begin in the middle of one side by taking a straight stitch over 4 threads and work into each thread round the outer square until the shape is complete (** or ***).

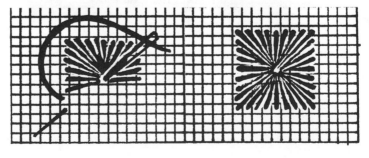

Small eyelet

Work as for square eyelet but only over 2 threads from the centre (** or ***).

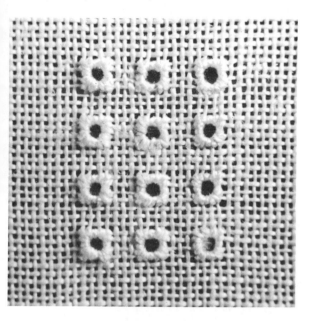

Single cross eyelet

Leave 1 thread between each quarter of a square eyelet
(** or ***).

Double cross eyelet
Leave 2 threads between each quarter of a square eyelet
and insert a stitch between the 2 threads (** or ***).

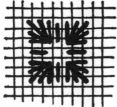

Star eyelet consists of 8 stitches from a central point, one to each corner, and one to the centre of each side, working round the square as for square eyelet. To make a filling, work in diagonal rows (**).

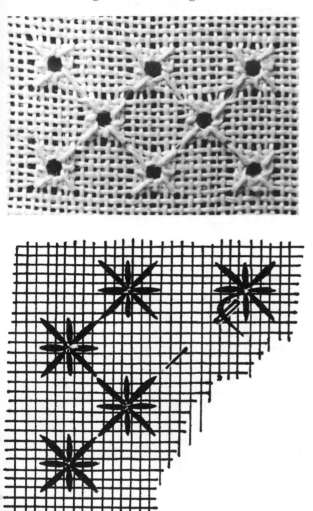

Round eyelet
Work round shapes as in other eyelets but count
threads from diagram (**).

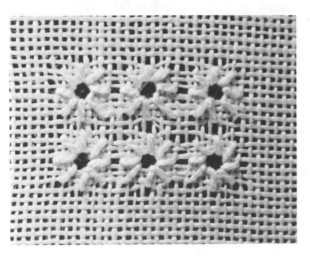

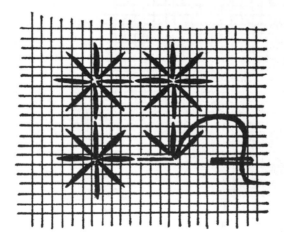

Hexagonal eyelet

Follow diagram for number of threads to go over and work 2 stitches into each hole. Work eyelets in diagonal rows to make a filling (***).

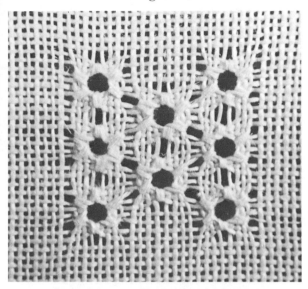

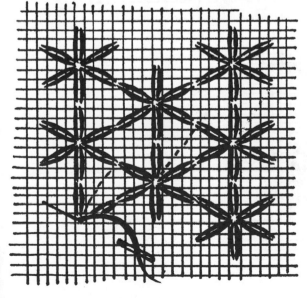

Diamond eyelet

Visualise a diamond shape 10 threads long and wide, and work round shape stitching into each diagonal hole (* or ***).

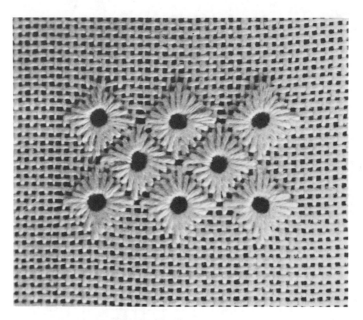

Free eyelets

An interesting and rich texture can be made giving a modern broken effect by working parts of eyelets or moving the hole to one side, and grouping them together (** or ***).

STITCHES BASED ON BACK STITCH
These stitches are all based on back stitch pulled tightly and each stitch is worked over twice.

Pulled back stitch is here worked over 3 threads.

These show a single line (***).

This illustrates 3 rows with 3 threads between the rows (***).

44

Festoon stitch is pulled back stitch in scalloped rows
which can be followed from the diagram (***).

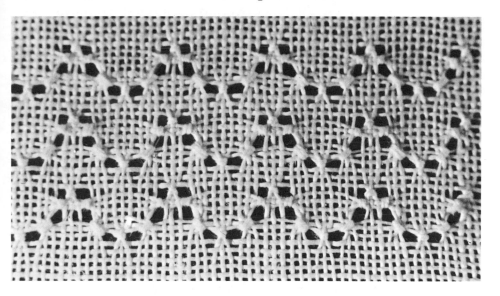

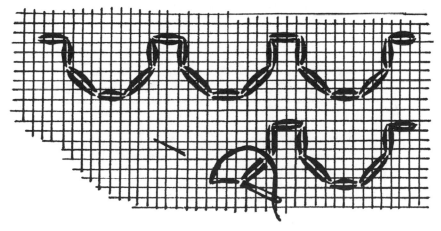

Ringed back stitch is precisely what its name suggests but is worked in a figure-eight movement (see diagram) and where the rows overlap on the return journey 4 stitches will use the same holes (***).

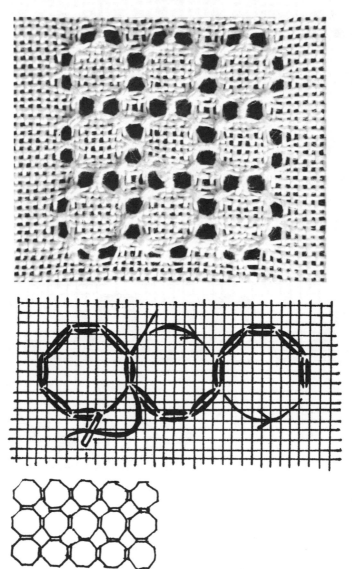

Frost stitch was invented by a student making an error when learning ringed back stitch, and thereby making an oval form. It may be worked in a figure eight or two rows (***).

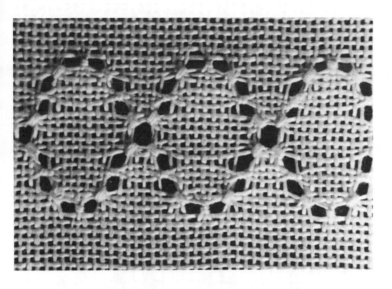

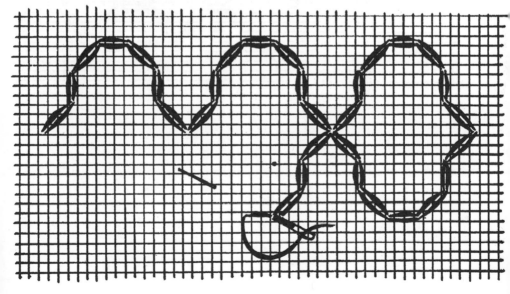

Small ringed back stitch
Having worked the previous stitches the diagram is
self-explanatory. Worked in two rows (***).

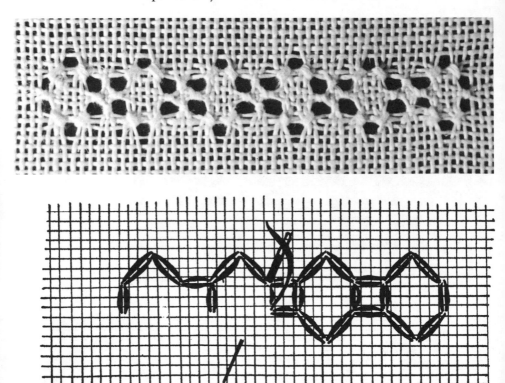

STITCHES BASED ON WAVE STITCH

Wave stitch
Although the stitches appear straight on the fabric when worked, they begin at an angle as can be seen from the diagram, and tight tension pulls them straight. Must be worked over even numbers of threads (***).

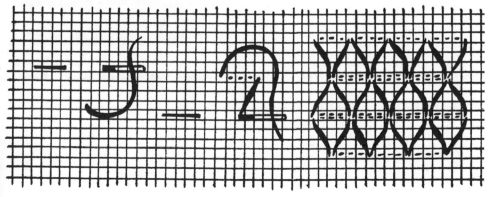

Reverse wave stitch
This stitch is exactly the same as wave stitch,
only the wrong side becomes the right side (***).

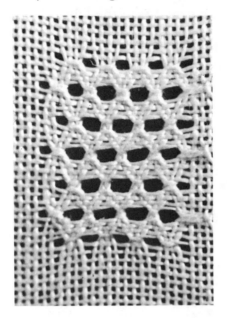

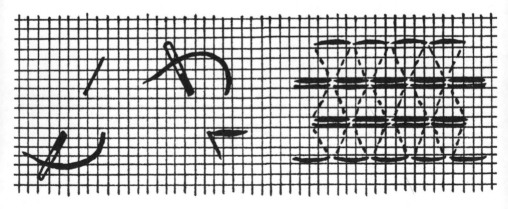

Double wave stitch

Each wave stitch is sewn over twice, giving a bolder effect than wave stitch (***).

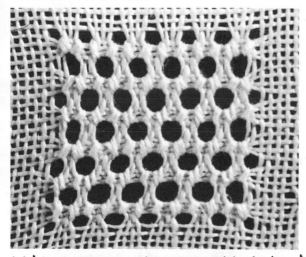

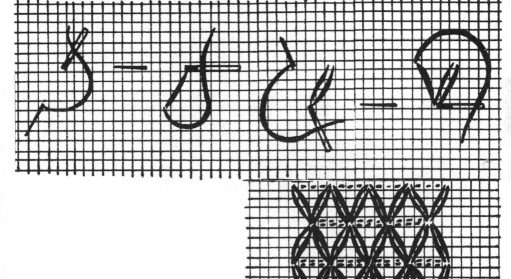

Window filling

This is a wave stitch worked over an uneven number of threads so that a single thread is left between the stitches, which forms the cross in the filling (***).

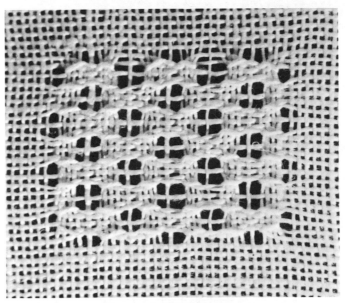

To START COME UP HERE

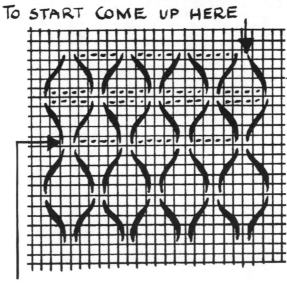

To BEGIN 2ND ROW COME UP HERE

Double stitch filling

This stitch is the reverse side of window filling and can be made one thread shallower in each row (***).

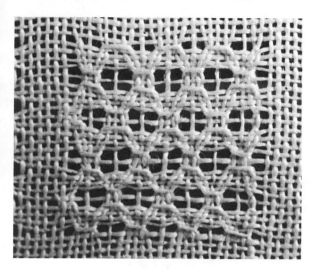

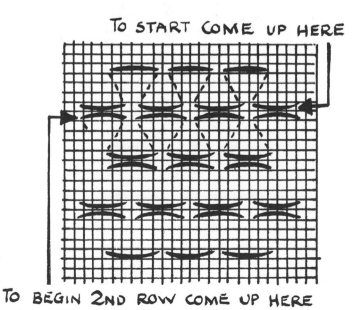

To START COME UP HERE

To BEGIN 2ND ROW COME UP HERE

Double window filling is a version of window filling where 2 threads are left between each stitch to form a grid (***).

BEGIN HERE

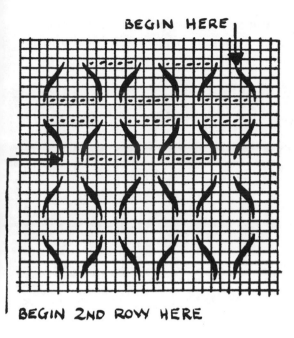

BEGIN 2ND ROW HERE

Waffle stitch has the same movement as wave stitch except that each stitch begins by being vertical and is slanted with tension (***).

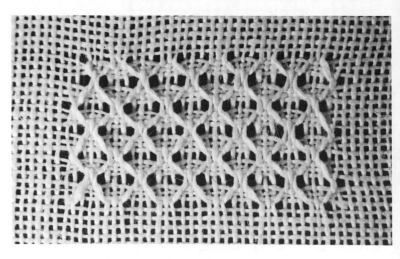

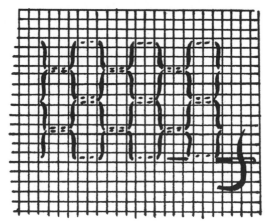

Honeycomb stitch is the same as waffle stitch except that a back stitch is taken over the horizontal threads. Best worked in a heavy thread (***).

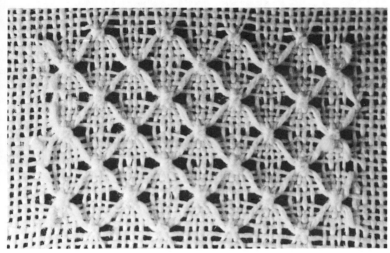

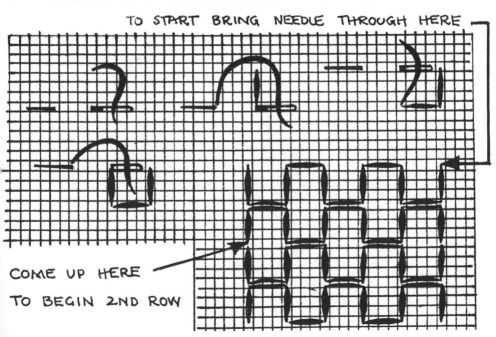

TO START BRING NEEDLE THROUGH HERE

COME UP HERE
TO BEGIN 2ND ROW

Cable stitch is a flattened version of reversed wave stitch; best worked in a thickish thread (**).

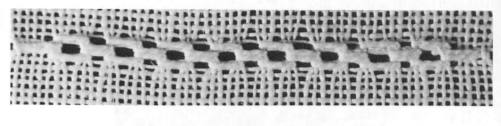

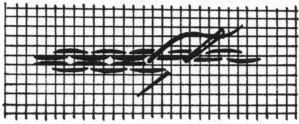

Pebble filling is also a version of reversed wave stitch except that a return row is worked over the spaces in the first row (**).

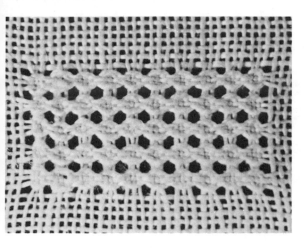

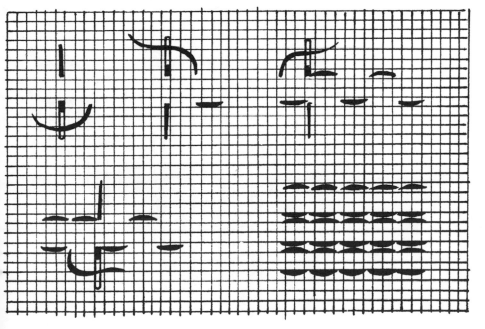

STITCHES BASED ON THE DIAGONAL

Although these stitches are effective on most materials, they may pucker the fabric unless it is loosely woven.

Single faggot stitch

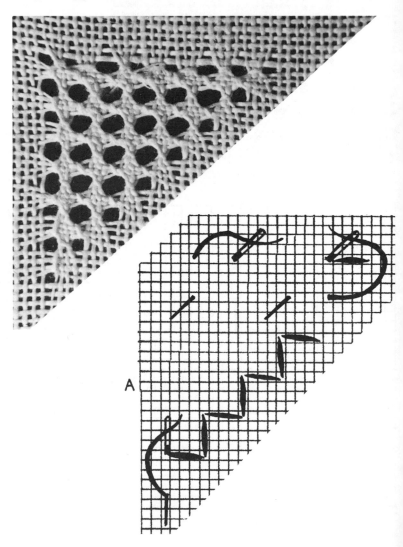

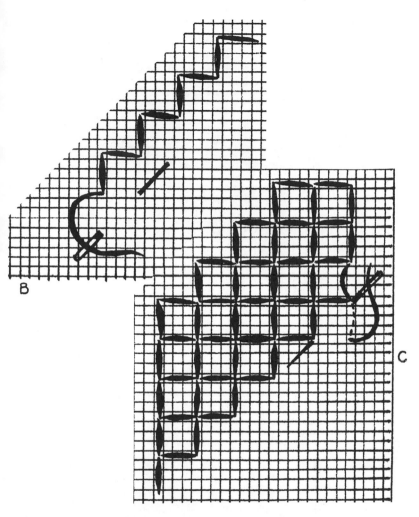

On the right side the stitches are straight on the fabric, and diagonal on the wrong side. 'A' shows the two movements of the stitch and 'B' how to turn. 'C' illustrates several rows of the stitch (***).

Reverse faggot is precisely what its name suggests and is the reverse side of single faggot (***).

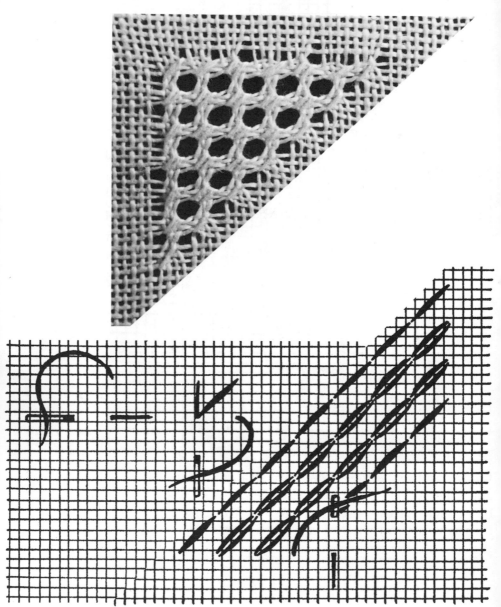

Diagonal drawn filling is single faggot stitch with a spacing of 1 thread between the rows (***).

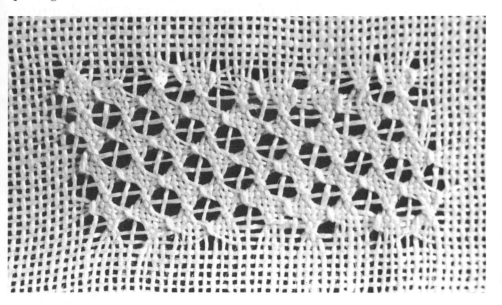

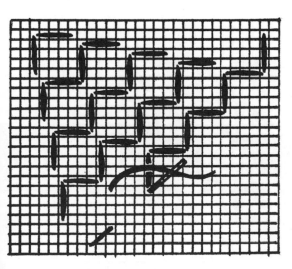

Mixed faggot stitch (diagonal chevron filling) consists of alternate rows of single faggot stitch and reverse faggot stitch. Most effective when worked in a thickish thread, particularly the rows of reverse faggot (*******).

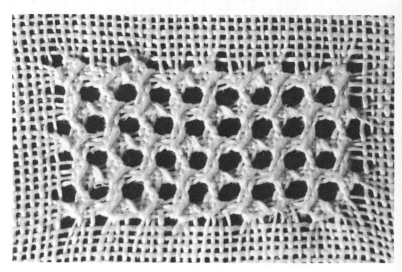

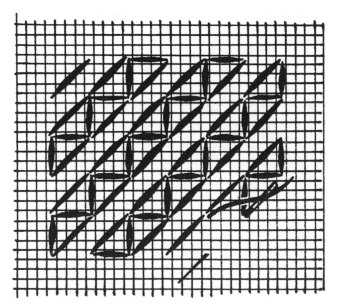

Drawn faggot filling (sometimes known as net filling). Although the diagram seems to have little relation to the photograph, this is how the stitch is worked. A large single faggot over 4 threads alternating with two rows of spaced single faggot over 2 threads (*******).

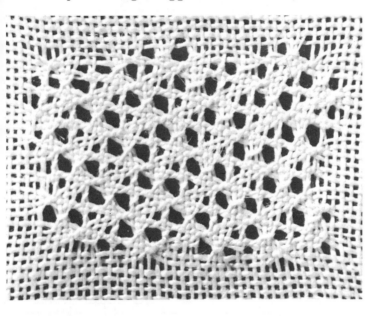

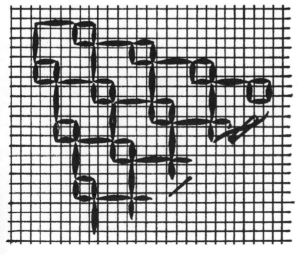

Double faggot is the same as single faggot except that each stitch is worked over twice. When finished it looks almost identical to a fine Russian drawn ground (***).

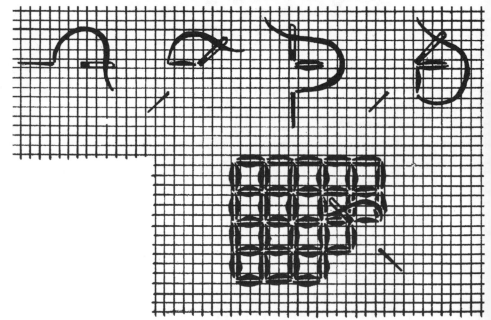

Diagonal cross filling is exactly what its name implies, but work all the half crosses in one row before coming back to complete the crosses. The rows are worked closely together (***).

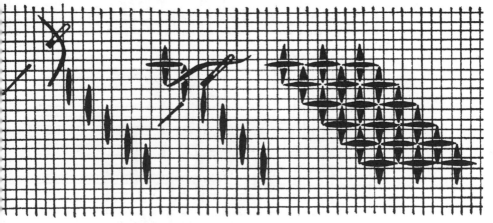

Diagonal raised band is worked in the same way as diagonal cross except the rows are spaced as in the diagram (***).

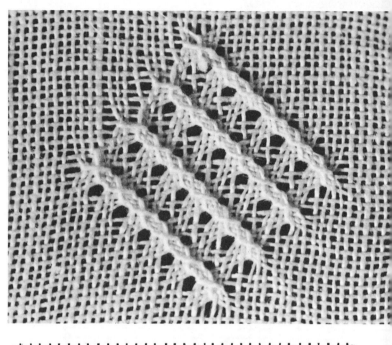

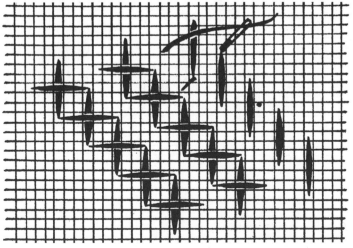

Open trellis filling

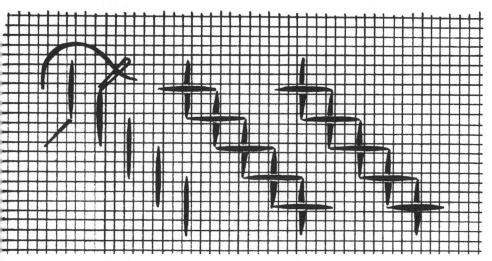

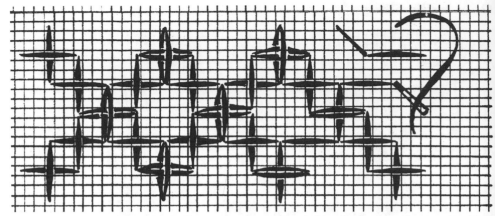

This stitch is another variation of diagonal cross filling. It begins by being rows of diagonal crosses spaced as in diagram on previous page. When they are complete, work the same stitch slanting the other way and crossing the existing stitches (***).

Detached square filling is the reverse side of open trellis filling (***).

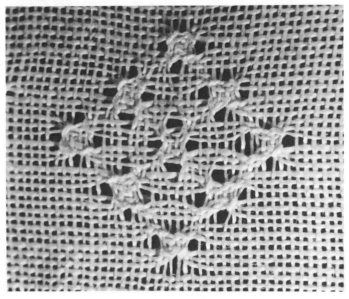

Crossed faggot filling

Work single faggot first and then work diagonal cross filling over it in thick thread (***).

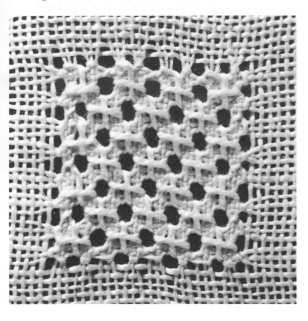

Chequer filling is similar to open trellis filling in that it is basically rows of cross stitch worked diagonally one way, then crossed by rows in the opposing direction. The lower diagram indicates the correct spacing (***).

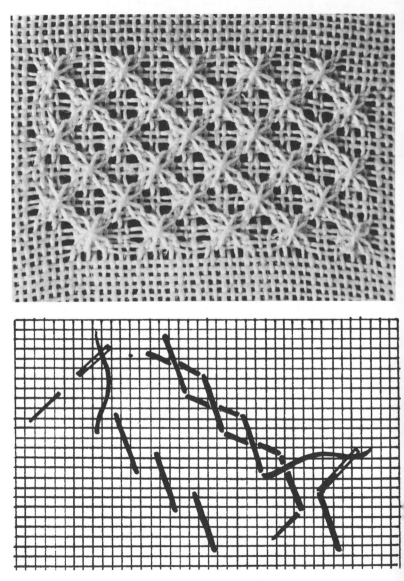

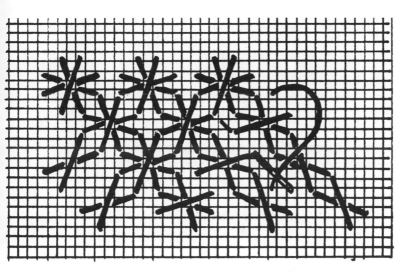

STITCHES BASED ON DOUBLE CROSS STITCH

The following stitches are all variations of double back stitch. One form of double back stitch can be worked freely on fine transparent materials when it is called 'shadow work', and on the wrong side it is closed herringbone stitch, so that it is extremely versatile. All these stitches are effective when worked on a loosely woven material because otherwise they can pucker the fabric. To see the threads clearly, double back stitch is best worked in a frame.

Basic double back stitch

Ripple stitch

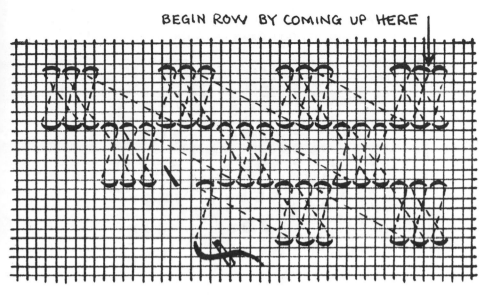

BEGIN ROW BY COMING UP HERE

This consists of alternate blocks of double back stitch and spaces, which are in bricked rows to form a filling. A long thread stretches from block to block on the wrong side, which can be lightly darned into the material if this stitch is used on a practical article (**).

Finnish stitch consists of blocks of double back stitch worked in stepped rows as in the diagram (***).

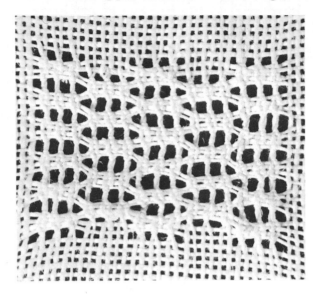

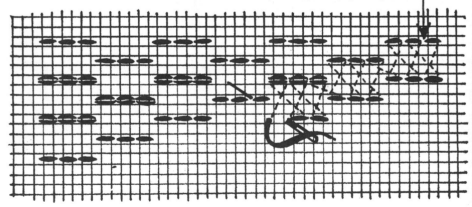

BEGIN ROW BY COMING UP HERE

Cushion stitch is formed from rows of oval blocks as shown, and takes its name from the tightly pulled ovals which look padded when worked (***).

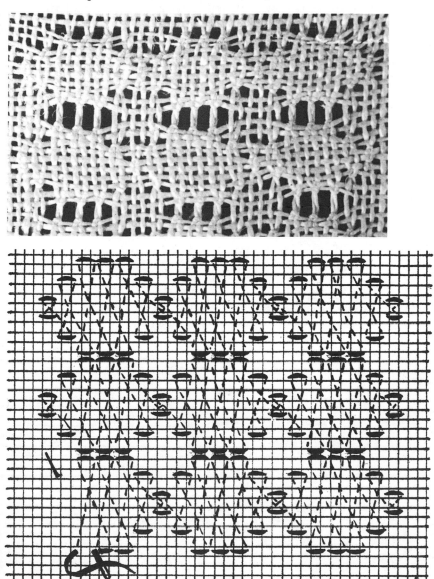

Diamond stitch needs a larger area in which to look its best, and consists of undulating lines worked over the same number of threads throughout. Once the stitch has been learnt, it is possible to vary the size of the diamonds by making the undulations shorter or longer (***).

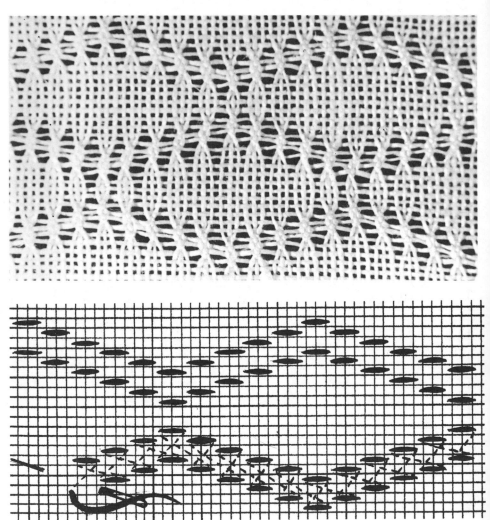

Triangle stitch is double back stitch sewn in a triangle, beginning as shown in the diagram. The stitch is worked in diagonal rows (***).

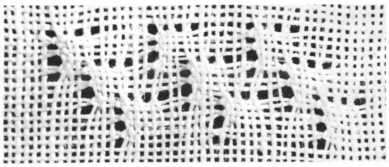

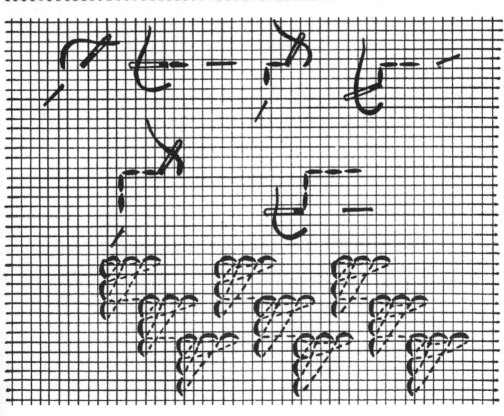

Square stitch can be worked in two ways: either work as for triangle stitch but continue the stitch to complete a square, which pulls the shape into a parallelogram, or work double back stitch round the shape, beginning at opposing corners and continuing in a clockwise direction, which pulls neat squares as in the photograph (***).

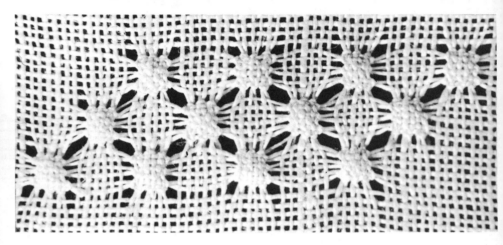

Braid stitch requires a large area to be seen at its best and should be worked on a frame, because the threads become distorted and confused otherwise (***).

TO BEGIN BRING NEEDLE THROUGH HERE

FILLINGS BASED ON GREEK CROSS STITCH

The following five fillings are all Greek cross stitch, the only difference being the spacing of the crosses. Below is a diagram of Greek cross stitch and all the fillings are worked in diagonal rows of this stitch.

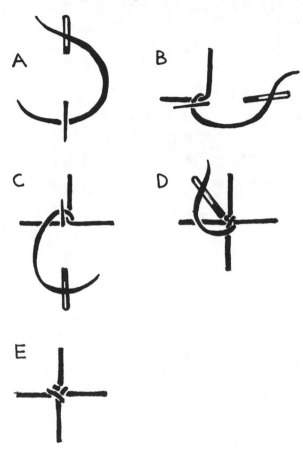

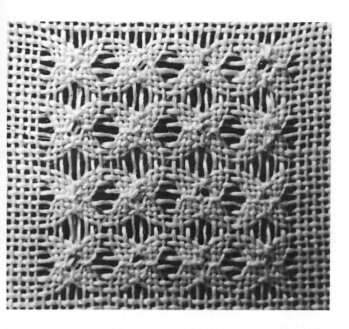

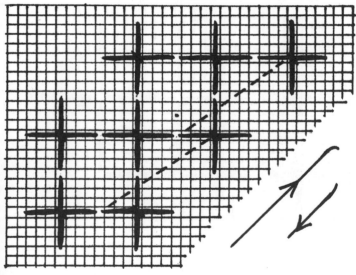

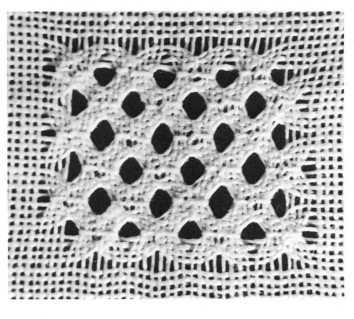

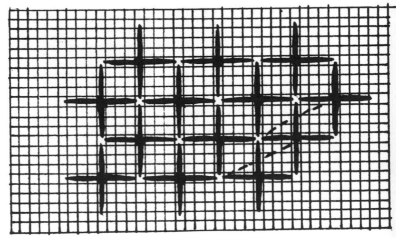

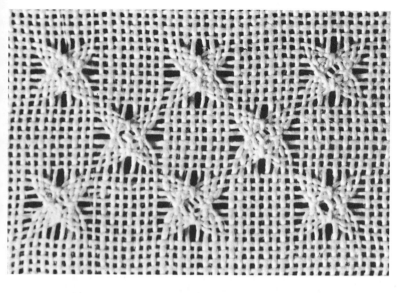

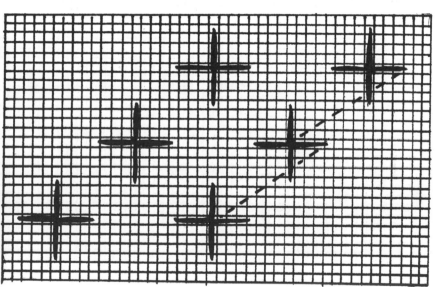

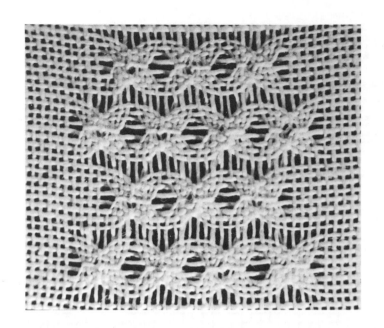

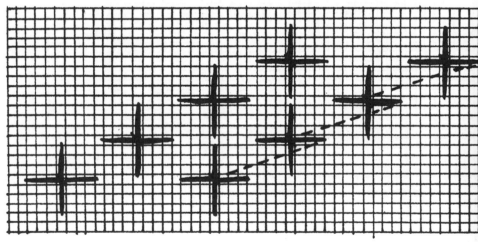

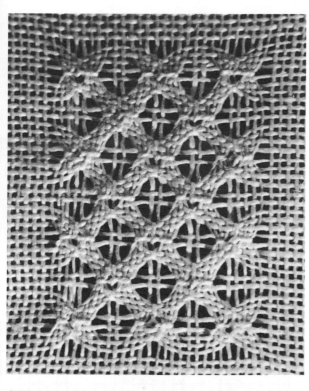

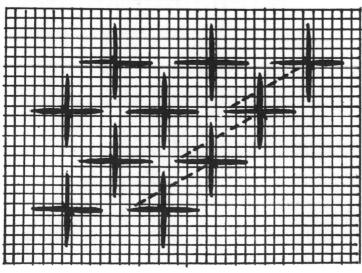

MISCELLANEOUS STITCHES

Indian drawn ground is worked in diagonal rows and the shape of the stitch is seen best on a fine openly woven material (***).

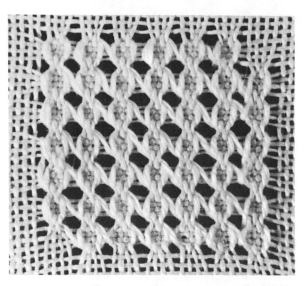

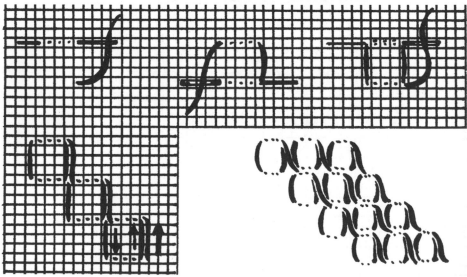

Drawn buttonhole is a form of buttonhole stitch worked on the counted thread. Two rows are worked back to back diagonally to form a ridge. Looks best in a twisted thick thread.

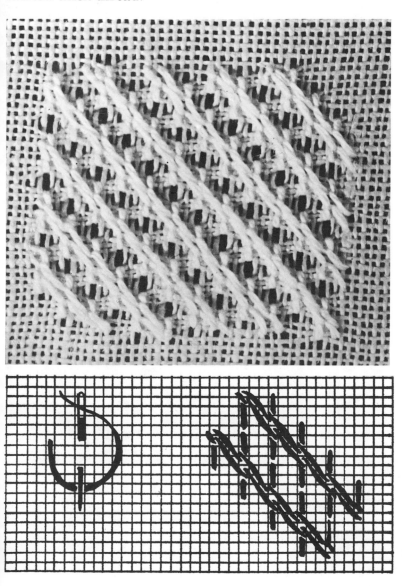

Rosette stitch

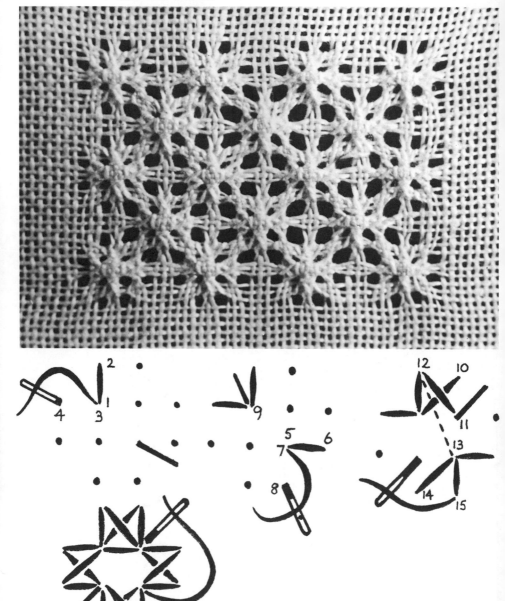

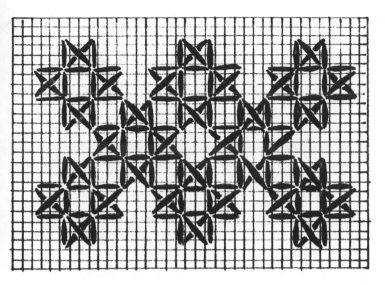

This is one of the most complicated stitches to learn,
especially from a diagram, and although it looks
effective when worked, chequer stitch has a similar
appearance and is less complicated. The numbers on
the diagram indicate order of working.

Four-sided stitch is a very versatile pulled stitch. Reading from A, the three movements are shown which build up each 'box' that forms the stitch. Note that the needle goes from corner to corner diagonally, making a cross stitch on the wrong side. B shows a method of turning a corner (*******).

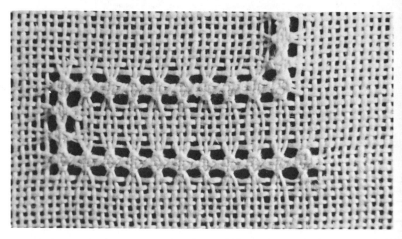

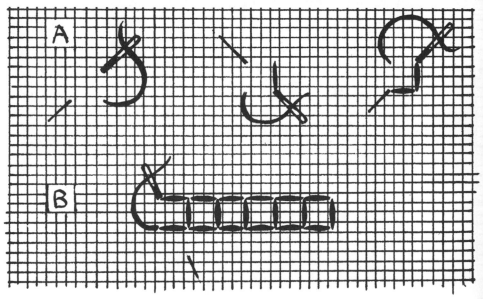

Three-sided stitch is a tricky stitch to master, but is
well worth learning because it can be both a line stitch
or a filling. Follow the movements shown in the
diagram and when completed each stitch is double
on the right side but diagonal stitches are single on the
wrong side (***).

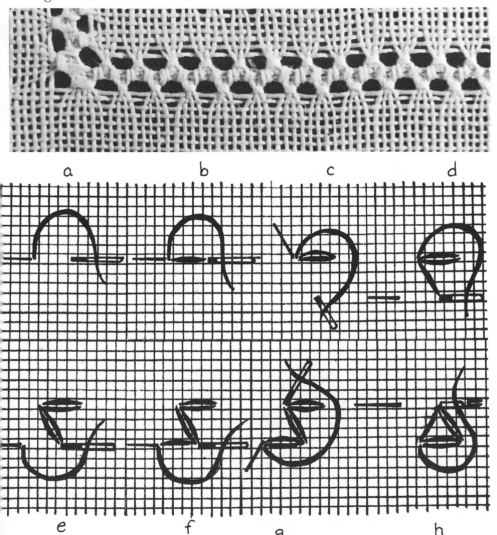

Eyelet stitch filling is a three-sided stitch worked in a circle from the same centre point to form an eyelet. Work in diagonal rows to make a filling.

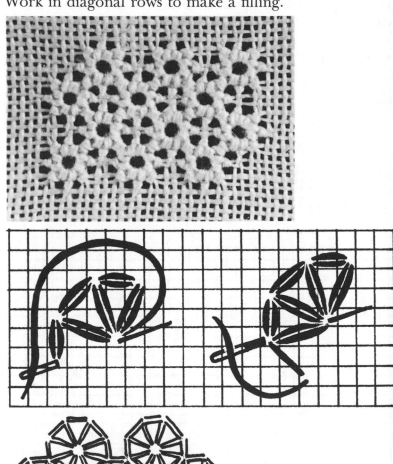

COMPOSITE STITCHES

Satin stitch and eyelet filling is exactly what its name suggests and can be followed from the diagram or illustration.

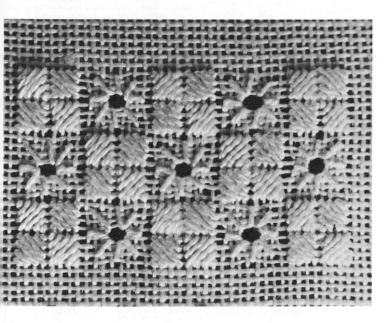

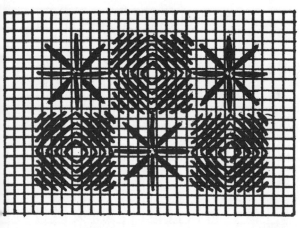

Diamond and spot filling

The diamonds are worked in either four-sided or single faggot stitch, with small satin stitch blocks in each.

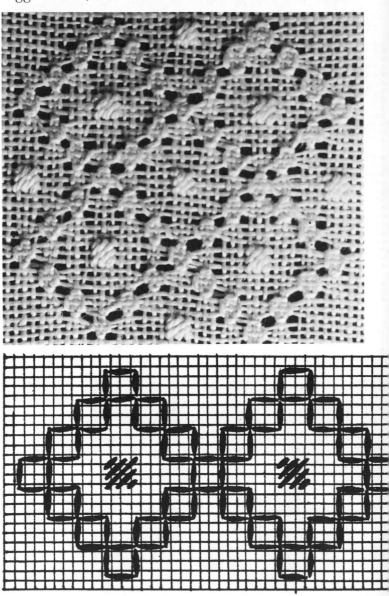

Greek cross and satin stitch filling

Satin stitch blocks are added to enrich a Greek cross filling.

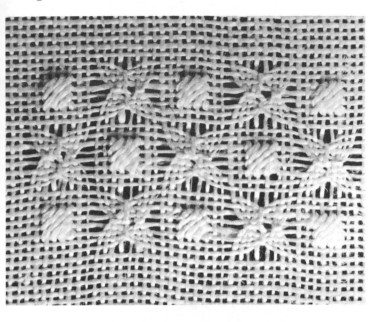

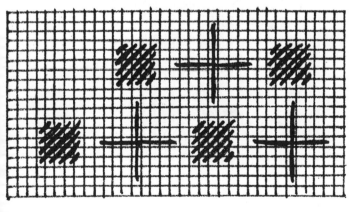

Four-sided stitch and satin stitch filling

A single four-sided stitch and 4 satin stitches are worked alternately to form a row, which is repeated in brick formation to make a filling.

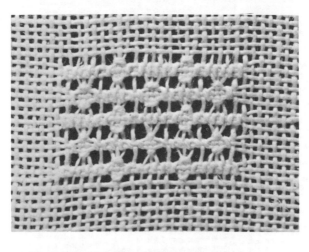

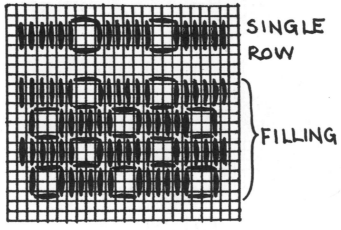

SINGLE ROW

}FILLING

Eyelet and step stitch filling
A step stitch of 6 stitches over 3 threads is worked, and the spaces filled with a square eyelet over 8 threads, giving a bold, rich texture.

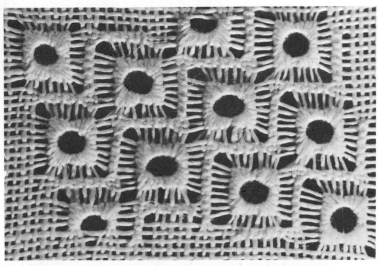

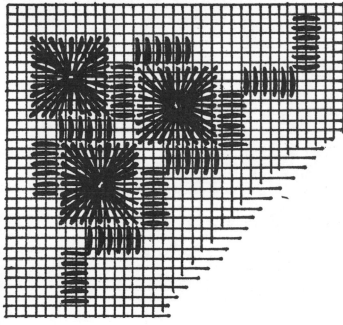

Outlined diamond filling

Diamond-shaped eyelets over 10 threads are separated by a diagonally worked satin stitch over 2 threads.

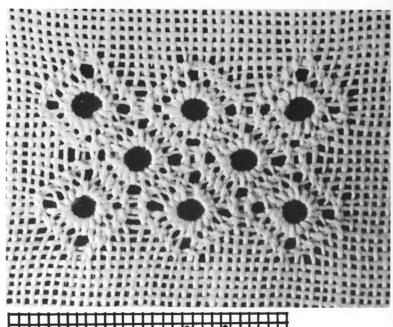

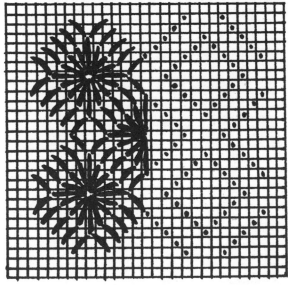

Thicket filling

Close rows of small square eyelets are worked over 4 threads alternating with 5 satin stitches over 2 threads (✳✳✳).

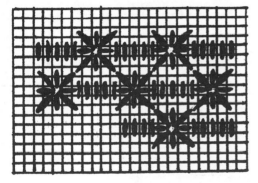

Reeded stitch

Close rows of 3 double back stitches over 5 threads, alternating with 5 satin stitches over 3 threads.

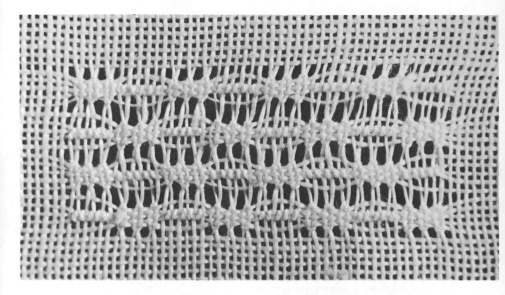

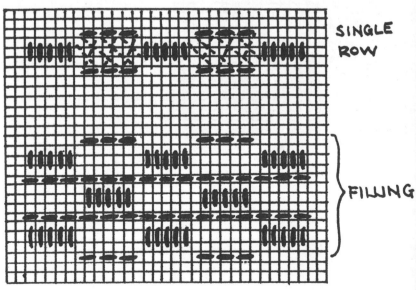

SINGLE ROW

FILLING

Mosaic filling

This is basically a square, bounded on each side by blocks of 5 satin stitches over 4 threads, in the centre of which a four-sided stitch is worked topped by a cross stitch. As well as forming a filling the squares may be used individually.

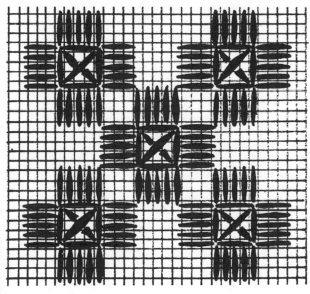

DESIGNING

To design for any method of embroidery it is necessary to understand the basic technique in order that its limitations are apparent. Pulled work is based largely on horizontal and vertical rows, so that if these lines can form the basis of a design the stitches will easily take their part in it. There is no one way of designing successfully, because it will depend to a great extent on the individual's personality and talent, but like any skill it has to be learnt and kept in practice. We do not expect to appear on the centre court at Wimbledon with only one tennis stroke, and yet many people are discouraged because they do not achieve a professional-looking design in one lesson.

Once a few basic stitches have been learnt, a limited design can be built directly on to the material, either as a border which could be applied in many practical ways, or 'freely' to form an experimental shape for either decorative or practical purposes.

The aim of the following pages is to show a beginner how to start, and to suggest some ways of designing so that by experiment it will be possible to develop confidence and an ability to see potential ideas in the shapes all around us in everyday life, for even a line of socks reflected as a shape in double glazing can be the basis of an apparently abstract design.

This satin-stitch motif could be used as a unit of
design which could be repeated to form decoration on
the mat below or continued as a border on bold
hessian to form the decoration for a cushion.

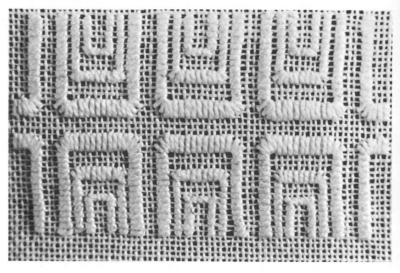

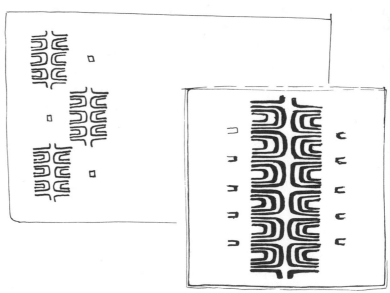

A simple border based on blocks of satin stitch, which
can be counted from the photograph. This could be
used on a bag of bold furnishing fabric or on a finer
material for a household article such as a tea cosy.

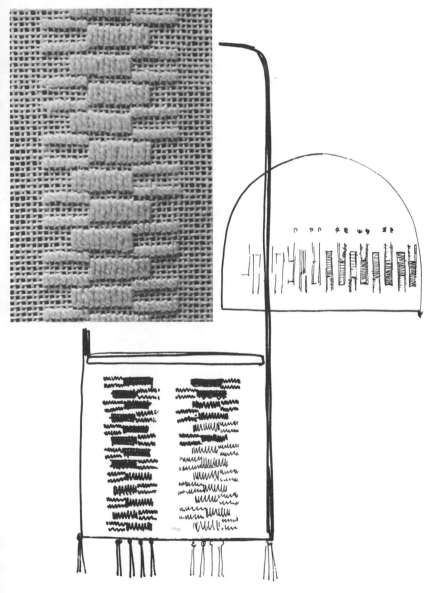

A border or unit of design based on satin stitch and diamond eyelets which could be worked finely for a collar and matching cuffs or on a coarser material to form the decoration round a box.

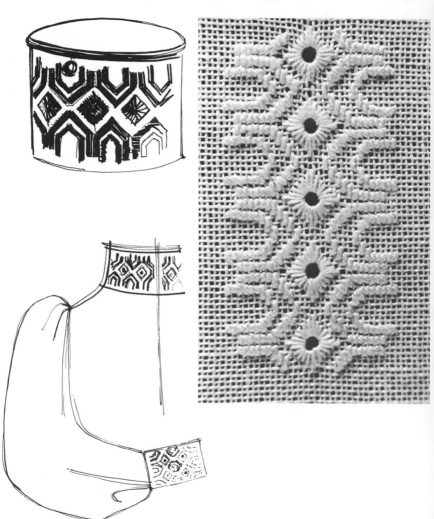

Three-sided stitch and satin stitch combine to form a border which has a feeling of movement. Worked very finely it could make an elegant pattern on a tie, or more boldly used, add richness to a pochette bag.

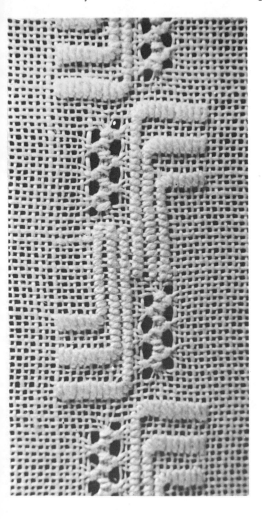

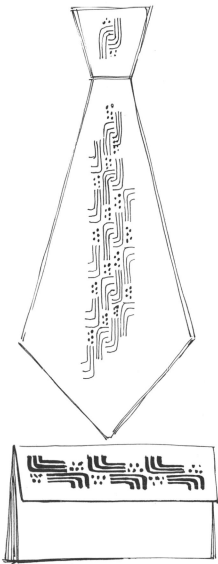

A narrow border in satin-stitch blocks and round eyelets could be repeated on the rectangular shape of mat or cushion, or used singly on a hair tie or band.

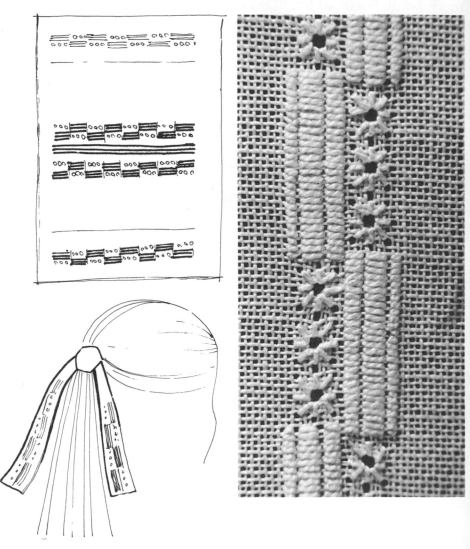

This border looks best on fine open material and could
be applied as a band round a lampshade or on
heavier material used to decorate a book mark.

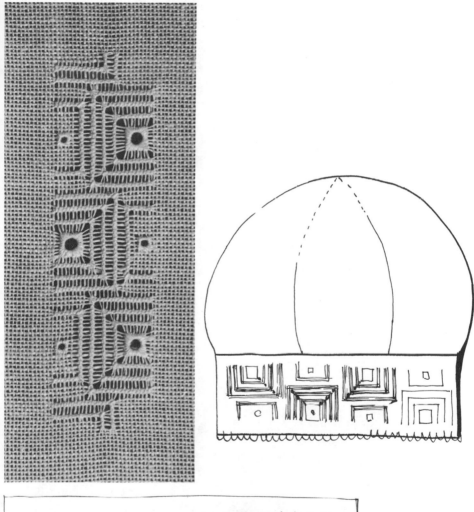

Three borders in satin stitch, combined with square eyelets, honeycomb stitch and oblong eyelets.

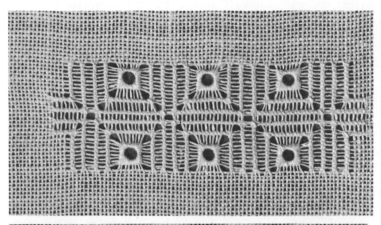

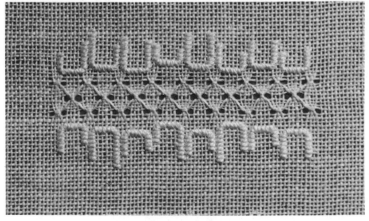

Corners of two conventionally worked napkins which are part of a set of four. By working each differently the working is made less tedious. Planned and worked by Mrs. Wakeling. Stitches used: eyelets, festoon, satin stitch and framed cross filling.

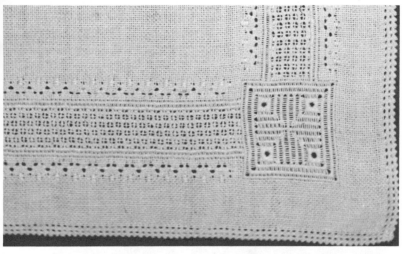

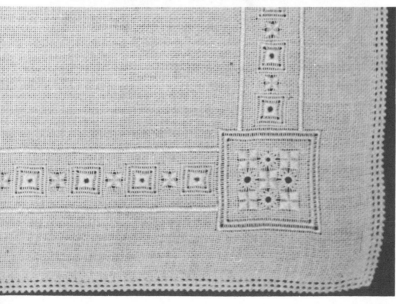

Two sides of the same lampshade in a red/pink/orange widely striped furnishing sheer; the pulled work was sewn directly on to the material after ascertaining exactly how much of the lampshade was seen at any one time. Stitches include eyelets, braid, Finnish and running.

Almost identical designs worked directly on to the material, illustrating the free use of pulled work. The mat is worked on white linen and the enlargement of the centre of another mat on scrim, incorporating satin stitch, eyelets and four-sided stitch. Designed and worked by Mrs. Edna Wark.

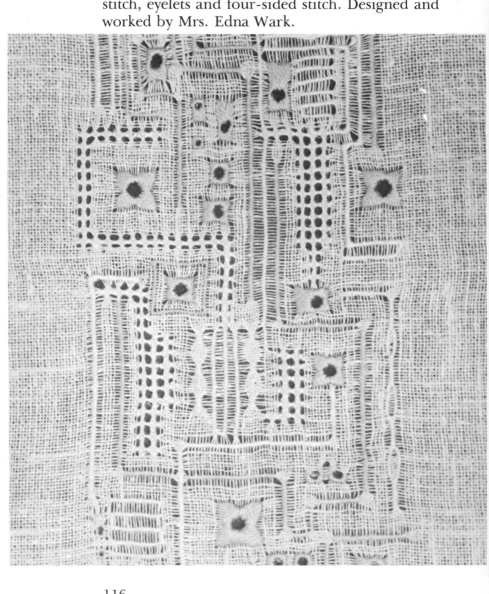

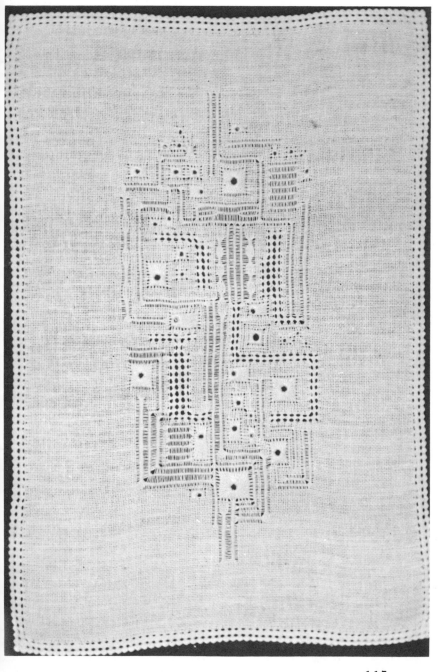

This flower is made up of three blocks of pulled fillings over which have been superimposed a free outline of Twilley's Bubbly knitting yarn which has added life and a feeling of movement. Twelve of these motifs, all slightly different, form the decoration on an attractive tablecloth, part of which is illustrated in the other photograph. Designed and worked by Mrs. Edna Wark.

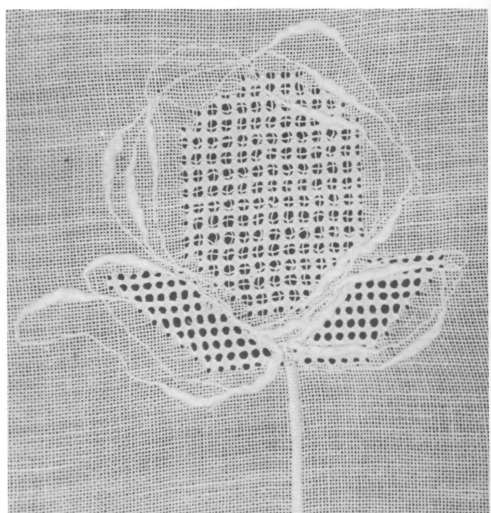

The two trees on this page were built up directly on to the material in satin stitch, the detail being added when the trees were complete.

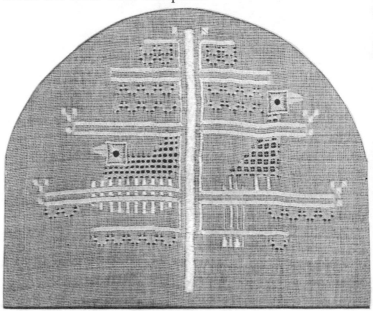

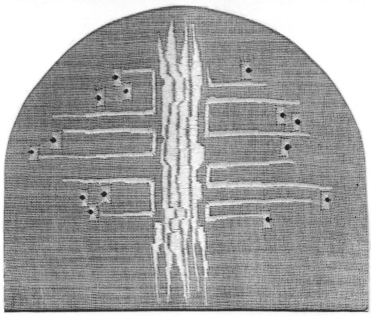

Part of a mat on pale green linen with simple white embroidery using satin stitch, honeycomb stitch and four-sided stitch with a picot edge, which because of its simplicity is very effective. Planned and worked by Mrs. Farrell.

These examples, all worked directly on to the fabric, were based on the same exercise in which the students were limited to 2 stitches, satin stitch and eyelets, and two thicknesses of thread. The schoolgirls are in their second year of embroidery only.

Helga Clarke worked this example, which resembles a stylised tree.

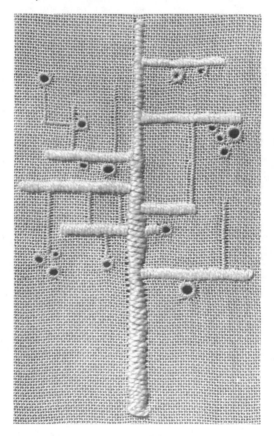

Opposite:
Hazel Crellin shows an unusual approach in working her example in black but mounting it on glittery paper to give it life.

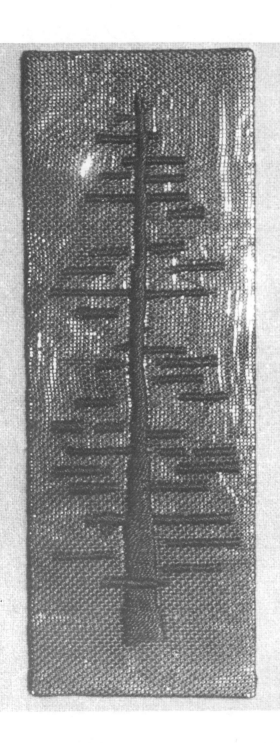

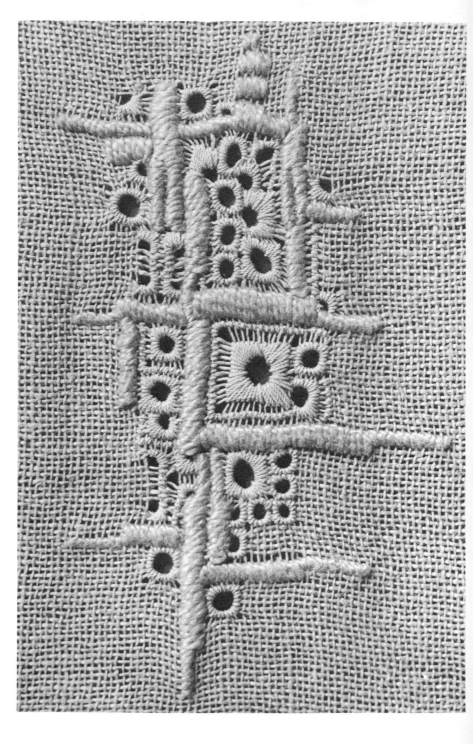

Opposite:
Mrs. Strafford is an experienced needlewoman and in her exercise has produced an attractive modern motif yet still retaining the competence of traditional techniques.

A sampler of free pulled shapes incorporating some needleweaving, by Alison Barrell.

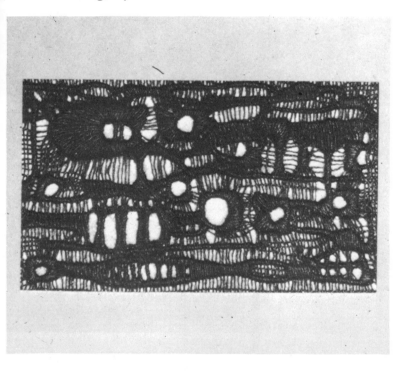

Overleaf:
The letter P worked in lines of four-sided stitch and both tensioned and loosely worked satin stitch. The upright lines are of unequal length to avoid giving too sharp and formal a shape to the letter.

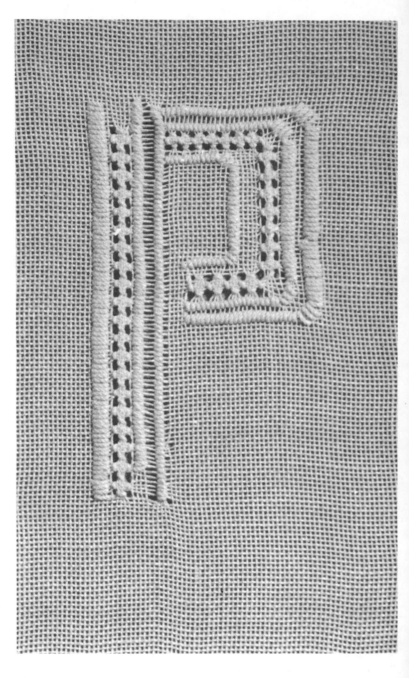

126

Most people, however lacking in confidence, are able to construct a grid, which can be tacked or worked directly on to the material in outline. The grid may be even or asymmetrical (below) or a loose construction of lines (below right) and may be interpreted in a variety of ways. The lines could be satin stitch, back stitch, four-sided or three-sided stitch, in fact any line stitch, though probably a smooth stitch would be the best foil for pulled fillings which can be used to texture some of the areas formed by the grid. The grid can be the basis of both practical and decorative items, from a pincushion to a large hanging.

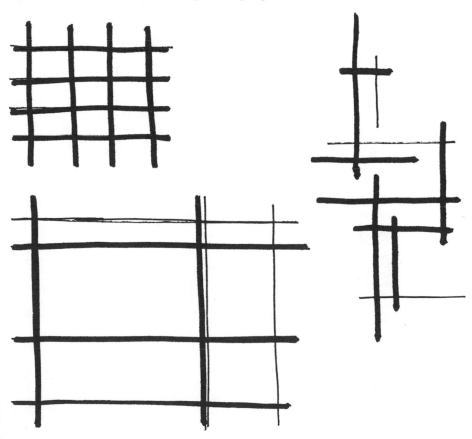

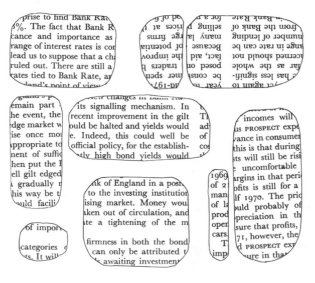

prices are,
mining th
ments, an
are likely
important
Where
ments? In
pay large
agricultur
should ov
output in
tion in th
may also
foodstuffs
advantage
probably
food consu
that the n
could be a
this Britai
imports a
On the
Britain a
expand m
effect of l

the first p
annual in
al fund.
r the years
Britain, wl
e volume
be increa
where Brit
s. Moreove
slow down
mption in l
et reduction
s much as
n would ha
mounting to
industrial
nd the Cd
ore rapidly.
igher prices

tent factor in deter-
demands and settle-
s angle, British costs
pidly than in other
countries.
the balance of pay-
Britain will have to
nts to the common
higher farm prices
It in increased farm
vill lead to a reduc-
od imports. There
exports of certain
as some productive
her food prices will
rate of growth of
n. PROSPECT believes
the food import bill
million, but against
pay levies on these
ut £200 million.
unt, trade between
on Market would
bearing in mind the
the spur which this

bably rise to about
d of the transition per
These strands in the ba
ummarized as follows.
he UK will be some
£500 million per ann
gements will be su
ment will build up
for example, the fir
may produce an
nts effect of about
verse effect may be
progression the m
in 1978.
interesting quest
could stand the st
The difficulties
l that the Comm
itain to make fr
Drawing Rights
IF arrangements
to the Comm
PECT believes th
ve important
period. ∎

The exploded shape is now well known as the basis for
design, the system being to cut into pieces of assorted
sizes any simple basic shape and move them apart.

prise to find Bank Rat
%. The fact that Bank R
cance and importance as
range of interest rates is cor
lead us to suppose that a ch
ruled out. There are still a
ates tied to Bank Rate, a
land's point of view.

g of pe
at prices
sums large firms
ppropriate to potential
voidup the improv
traders
ands mer spent
1961-19

for a
selling
many la
Because
fact, aid
be posed
be consti
year

Bank Rate
from the Bank of
number of lending
nge in rate can be
not should concerned
far as the whole
has less signifi
to make again

emain part
he event, the
dge market w
ise once mo
ppropriate to
nent of suffi
hen put the
ell gilt edged
gradually r
his way be t
uld facili

its signalling mechanism. In
recent improvement in the gilt
uld be halted and yields would
e. Indeed, this could well be
official policy, for the establish-
tly high bond yields would

nk of England in a pos
to the investing institution
ising market. Money wou
ken out of circulation, and
te a tightening of the m

firmness in both the bond
can only be attributed t
awaiting investmen

of impor
categories
ts. It wil

incomes will
s PROSPECT exp
ance in consumer
this is that during
ts will still be ris
uncomfortable
rgins in that peri
ofits is still for a
If 1970. The pri
uld probably of
preciation in th
sure that profits,
71, however, the
d PROSPECT ex
ure in tha

1969
of 2
man
of la
prod
oper
cars.

128

Attention should be paid to the background shapes that emerge and not only the shape of each section of cut paper. On the left are two shapes exploded from a square, the top one having been cut vertically and the other one both horizontally and vertically, after which the shapes were rounded. This suggested an interesting background shape, and the photograph shows an interpretation of the design by working single faggot stitch on a curtain fabric in different sizes in the background area.

Another version of the exploded shape based on an oblong. The design has been purposely made slightly irregular to avoid exact repetition, which would be boring to work and look at. The interpretation in embroidery shows a subtle use of pulled work; stitches

130

used are festoon, ringed back, Greek cross, reeded, Finnish and satin stitch on a deep rose-red furnishing fabric. Designed and worked by Miss Diana Dalmahoy.

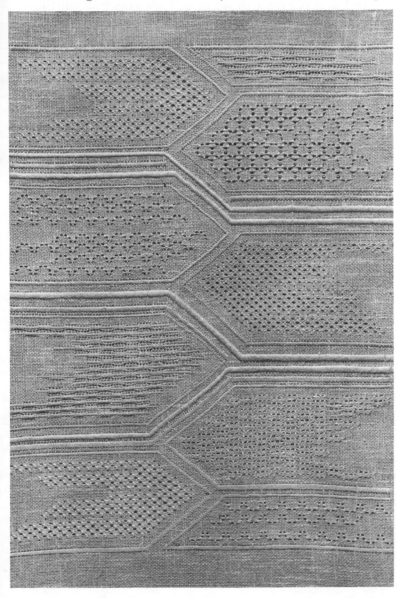

A circle is the basis of this exploded design seen in cut paper and embroidery; as well as pulled thread techniques an area of encroaching Gobelin has been worked as a contrast in texture. Free couched outlines have been superimposed on the design to link the basic shapes; the ground is emerald green Moygashel and on it are worked matching threads of Anchor Soft, *coton à broder* and stranded cotton.

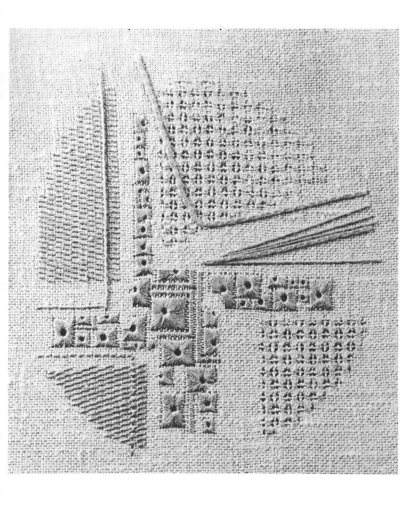

133

Natural forms may also be exploded; in these examples paper shapes were cut from actual leaves and segmented to make further shapes. It is interesting that many exploded leaves suggest flower shapes.

This design was based on actual leaf shapes which have become formalised by their simple decorative treatment. Stitches used on a dark brown linen are ringed back, ripple, tensioned satin and buttonhole, wave, double back and encroaching Gobelin. Designed and worked by Mrs. Jennifer Frost.

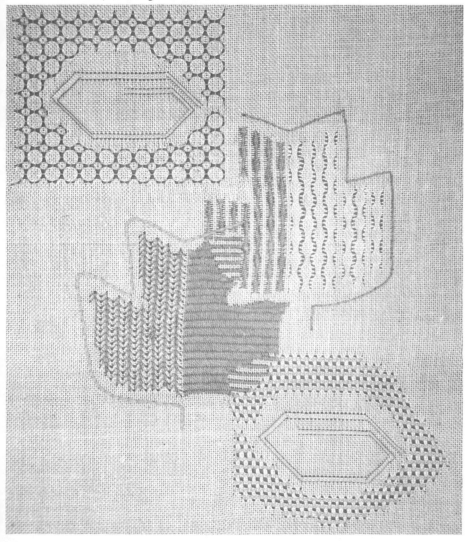

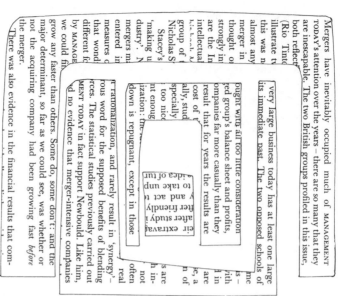

These are not true exploded shapes but are all cut from a basic square from which some pieces have been removed. They could be used to decorate a book cover, enlarged for a cushion, mat or panel, or increased further in scale for a hanging.

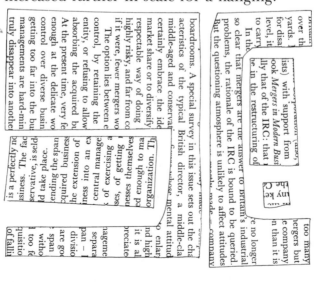

136

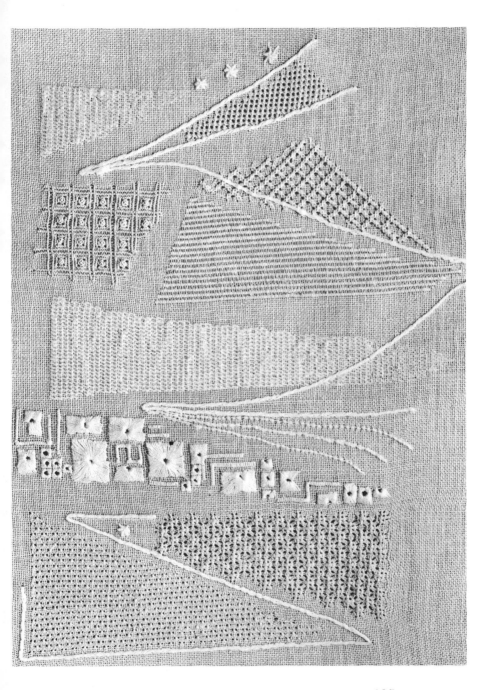

Previous page:
A tray cloth based on cut paper shapes by a worker who had not previously attempted modern pulled thread but had a sound basic technique. Designed and worked on white linen by Mrs. Akers.

Linear doodles based on horizontal and vertical lines are another suggestion for beginning a design and ideas can be derived from town planning maps, wiring circuits or technical drawings. Despite being linear they enclose geometric areas particularly suited to pulled thread fillings. Such a design can be planned directly on to material by pinning thread or string to shape on the fabric, and then the basic outlines can be made both subtle and interesting by thoughtful use of varied stitchery as is suggested by the different thicknesses of line in the illustrations.

139

As lettering is essentially a linear craft it is particularly difficult to translate into acceptable terms for pulled thread, but it is not impossible. If lettering is to be read it must be clearly legible, but letters may also be combined to form a unit of design for use on personal objects; box top, belt or tie, for example.

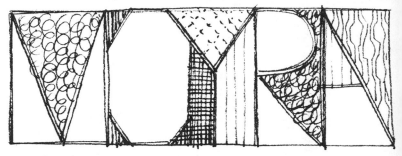

On this page are shown three ideas for lettering in pulled work based on short names, and initials could be similarly used. In 'Moyra' the background divisions form the letters, which need only thin outlining with pulled fillings worked between them. 'Pam' is entirely linear so would be worked in close rows of line stitches such as satin, back and double back, three- and four-sided. A closely worked stitch, such as double faggot, would form the background of 'Gay', leaving only a minimal outline to be sewn.

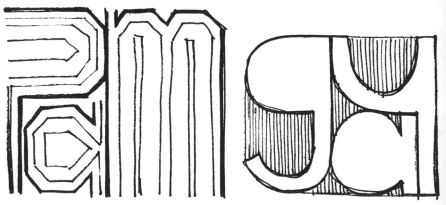

140

The design of the mat is based on the name 'Brian' and is worked on white linen in satin stitch (used vertically and horizontally) in thick thread contrasted with bold areas of fillings. The hem is wide in order to frame the design.

A quotation could form the basis of a design for church embroidery, which the sketch illustrates, the angular shapes being dictated by the method.

Natural forms such as birds, fish and plants can be reduced decoratively into very simple shapes and yet still be recognisable. On these pages are designs of birds made up of vertical, horizontal and diagonal lines enclosing geometric areas that will readily translate into pulled thread. Other subject matter already based on geometric forms are buildings, from stately homes and churches to small houses, ships of all ages, and machinery.

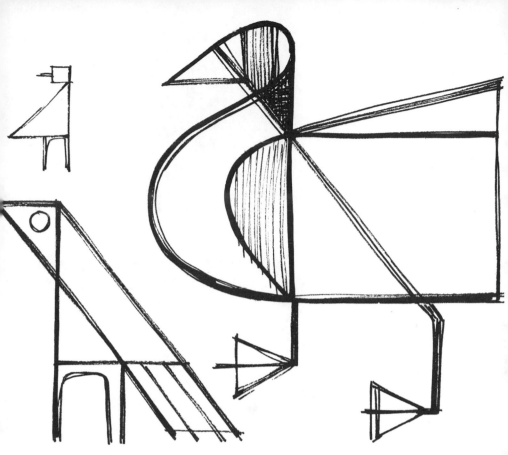

Overleaf left:
'Drumnadrochit'; a panel of a fish in a combination of
techniques including appliqué, surface stitchery, pulled
thread, with some mica and shisha glass. The whole
panel is in rich colours of wine red on a deep blue
striped furnishing fabric using a wide selection of
threads. Designed and worked by Mrs. Ryrie.

Overleaf right:
A very stylised peacock forms the basic design of this
sampler which was among the prizewinners in an
international sampler competition in 1967. Both cream
coton à broder and olive green stranded cotton are used
on an off-white linen to show a variety of fillings.
Designed and worked by Mrs. Monica Spanton.

143

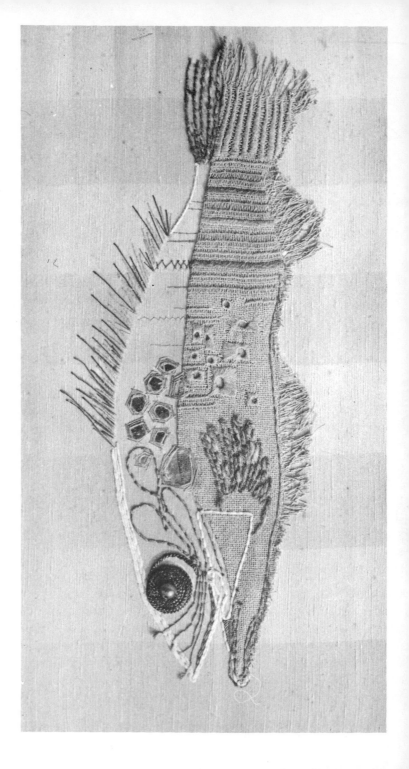

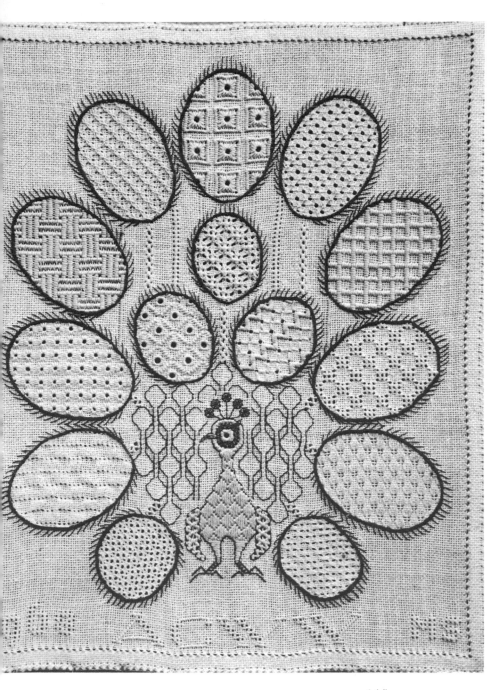

145

Two sections of a panel by M. Cole incorporating an inventive combination of pulled and drawn thread work and padded appliqué on white in shades of blue.

Opposite:
Panel in builder's scrim illustrating a vigorous use of free pulled thread in combination with other techniques. Designer/executant Alison Barrell.

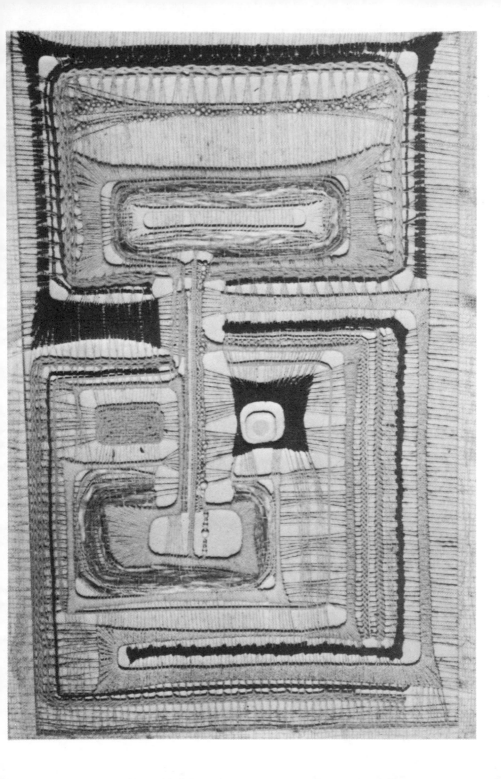

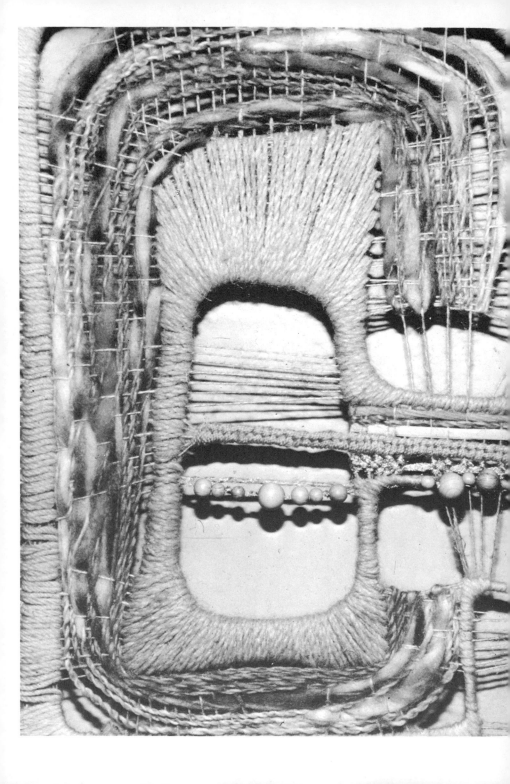

Opposite:
An enlargement of part of the previous panel clearly illustrating the use of surface stitchery, darning and beads in conjunction with a magnificently bold eyelet hole.

Below:
Thickly grouped dark red warp threads are stretched in front of a richly coloured and textured ground, and although this panel is not true pulled thread it does suggest a direction for further experiment. Designer/executant Margery Self.

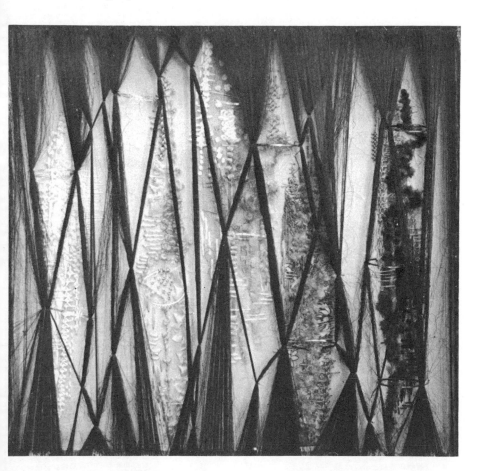

Opposite:
This photograph from Japan of beer crates in a yard
was taken from a helicopter at such an arresting angle
that it has become an abstract design; because of the
geometric shapes, translation into a counted thread
method is immediately suggested. In many similar
ways, actual objects can be the root of 'abstract'
designs. (By courtesy of the Press Association.)
Below:
'Rock Pool' is an imaginative amalgam of techniques in
a three-dimensional panel. The top surface is window-
cleaner's scrim with cut and pulled eyelets, shapes
padded and satin-stitched or whipped, surrounding a
large hole through which is seen an area of texture
underneath. Designer/executant Pat Wood.

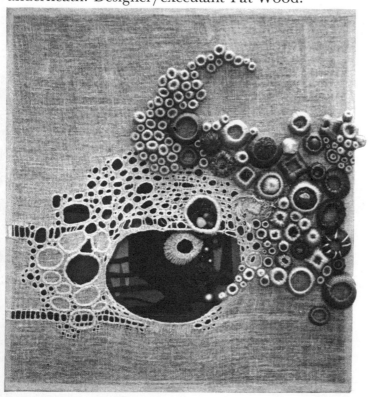

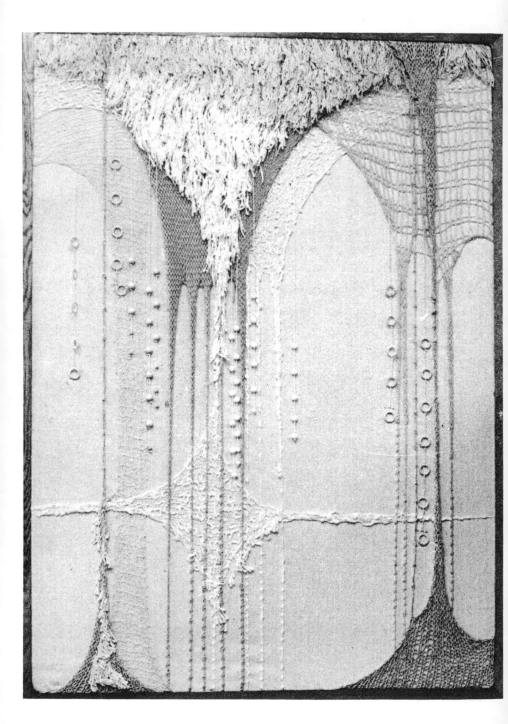

Opposite:
This panel illustrates a new idea of pulling. A fabric is formed, in this instance by knitting, and is pulled to shape and attached to a background. The shapes here suggest architectural forms and have been enriched with beads, fringed Twilley's Bubbly and covered rings. The panel is in muted colours of pink, brown and off-white. Designer/executant Margaret Gabay.

Overleaf left:
Part of a hanging in builder's scrim demonstrating that movement and life can be achieved in pulled thread by bold designing. Free pulled thread is worked with wool, string, flax and unwoven ground threads, together with some fringing and plaiting which combine to make a most satisfying and lively hanging. Designer/executant Barbara Siedlecka.

Overleaf right:
A richly coloured and textured panel incorporating a variety of techniques, including pulled thread, in a 'layer' design suggesting rock formation. Designer/executant Alison Barrell.

153

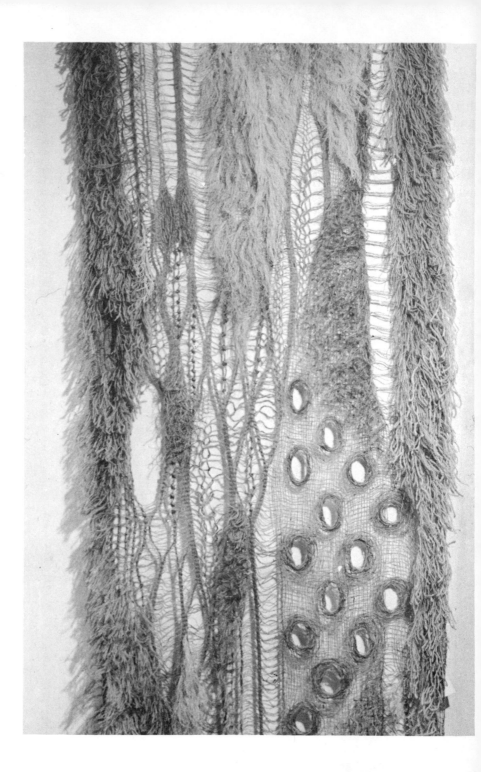

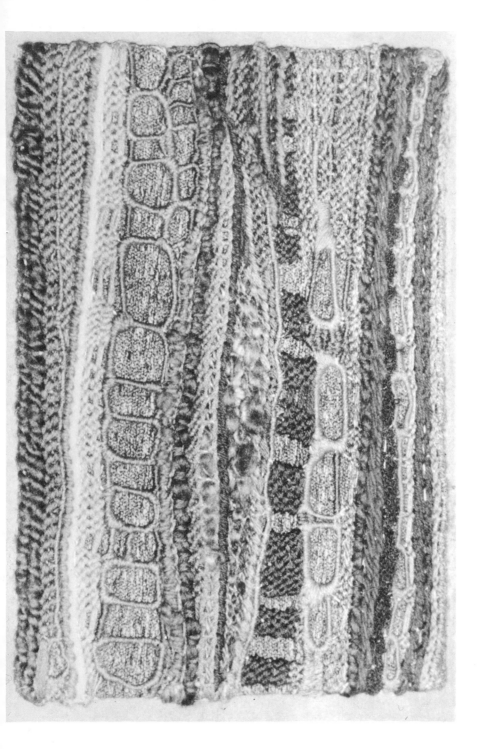

EDGINGS

Because pulled work is particularly suitable for utilitarian articles of dress and household linen, many edgings have been evolved based on pulled thread stitches, but they should always be considered as an integral part of the overall design of an article. An eye-catching edging can detract from the rest of the embroidery or even cause a confused and muddled effect because the article has been over-elaborated. If the edging is rich and interesting this might prove sufficient decoration for some items, leaving the rest of the article completely plain to show it to best effect.

If it is intended to combine an edging with other embroidery the edging should be considered and worked last, when it will be more obvious what is required; simply leave plenty of material to allow for its formation. There can be no set rules for width of hem as this will depend on many factors – purpose, weight of fabric, boldness or otherwise of the rest of the design – and the choice rests on individual judgment and selection.

Corners can be a problem, and it is well worth learning to mitre a corner well, although in Scandinavian work corners are not often mitred and yet they look neat.

In the following pages are just a few permutations on the theme of pulled thread edgings, concentrating on

157

the actual finishing of the edge rather than rich decoration which could be formed by adding borders to edgings.

HOW TO MITRE A CORNER
A mitred corner is stitched on the cross and the most important point is to handle the material as lightly as possible to avoid stretching.

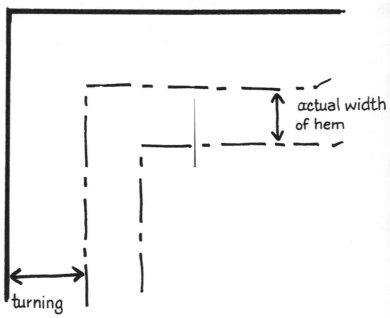

actual width of hem

turning

allow width of hem plus ⅜″ (8mm)

Mark final hem lines in tacking to begin, exactly on the thread of the material.

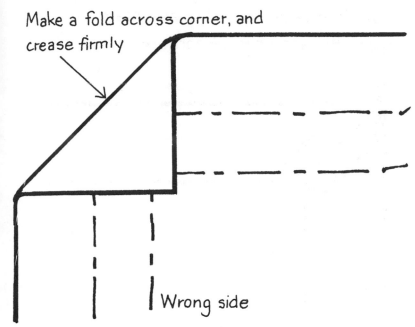

Make a fold across corner, and crease firmly

Wrong side

Be very careful not to stretch the material when making the diagonal crease.

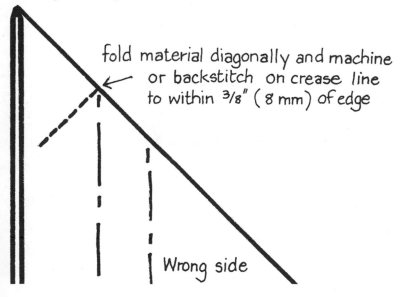

fold material diagonally and machine or backstitch on crease line to within 3/8" (8 mm) of edge

Wrong side

Cut off excess material, press seam
open flat and snip off corners

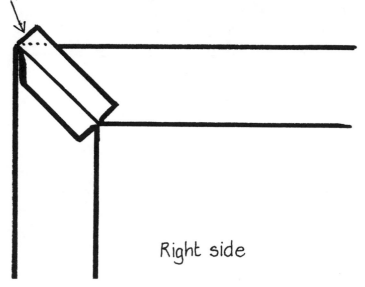

Right side

Turn hem inside out so that it lies
on the wrong side
Turn edge under and stitch in position

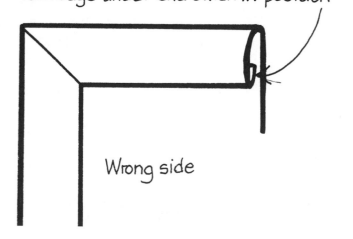

Wrong side

Simple faced edge: cut a piece of material for facing from fine linen or cotton exactly the same size and shape as the embroidered piece. Put article and facing right sides together and tack and machine on finished hem line, leaving about 3" (8 cm) unstitched, in the middle of one side. Trim corners, turn through to right side and slip stitch opening together. After a light press the edge may be secured by a row of stitching about $\frac{3}{8}"$ (1 cm) from the edge. This method is particularly suitable for place mats as the facing forms an extra layer for heat resistance.

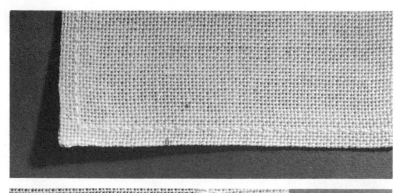

This edge makes a broad, frame-like edging and is wide in proportion to the whole article, whether mat or cloth. Leave $\frac{1}{2}"$ (1·5 cm) in addition to hem-turning allowance. Mitre corners but do not turn under edge.

Tack hem in position and work a broad counted satin stitch through both layers of fabric from the right side. To secure hem finally work a row of back stitch or double running stitch about 3 or 4 threads on the outer side of the satin stitch. Lastly trim off excess material on the wrong side close to the satin stitch.

Although much narrower, this hem is worked in a very similar way to the previous one, the hem being secured by two rows of satin stitch worked side by side and pulled fairly tightly; the excess material is trimmed off on the wrong side only when both rows of satin stitch are completed.

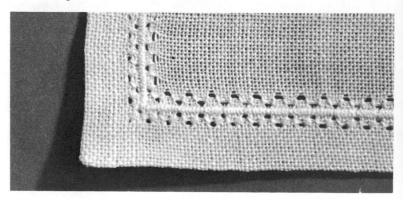

This hem is begun in the same way as the previous two, but when a row of satin stitch is completed, work a row of double wave stitch on the outer side of the satin stitch, trim off any excess material on the wrong side and work another row of double wave stitch on the inner edge.

Hem-stitched hem: mitre corners and tack hem in position exactly on the grain of the material. A thread may be withdrawn before beginning the hem stitch, though there is the opinion that this weakens the hem if the article is to be laundered frequently.

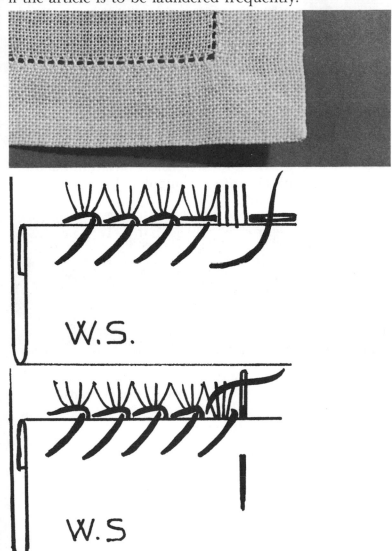

W.S.

W.S

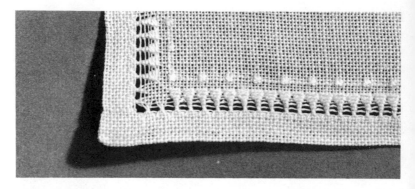

A hem-stitched hem with satin-stitch decoration. The hem stitch is worked over 4 threads and the satin stitch over the same groups of threads, with small satin-stitch spots over every other block. Tension variation makes the satin-stitch blocks into a triangular shape.

Another hem-stitched hem, after which three-sided stitch is worked over the same groups of threads and a row of honeycomb stitch next to the three-sided stitch.

PICOT EDGINGS

The following picot edgings are only three of many ways in which these edgings may be made. By removing a thread before working the first line of stitching in any of the methods a sharper picot will be formed.

Picot edge 1

Three satin stitches are worked over 4 threads tightly in a consecutive line, marking the finished edge of the article.

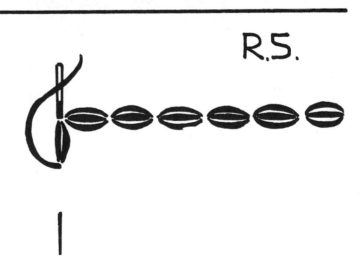

Fold material over so that the stitches are exactly on the edge of the fold and work thus:

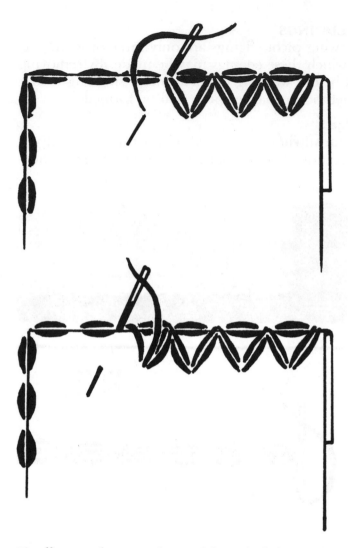

Finally turn hem under and hem lightly on the wrong side.

Picot edge 2

Work 4 buttonhole stitches over the same 4 threads, pulling tightly, and continue in this manner along a line marking the finished edge of the article.

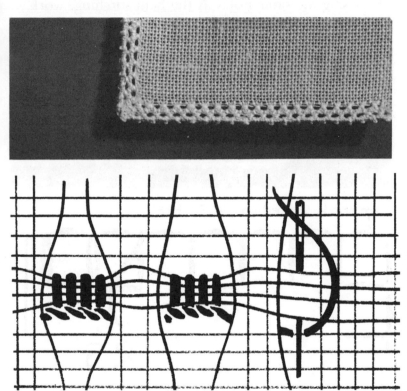

Fold material over so that buttonhole picots are on edge of fold and work three-sided stitch through both layers of material from the right side. Trim off raw edge close to three-sided stitch on the wrong side.

Picot edge 3

Begin by working hem stitch tightly on the wrong side of the material over about 4 threads. Fold material over so that the horizontal stitch lies on the edge of the fold. Using the same holes as the hem stitching, work the following stitch through both layers of material.

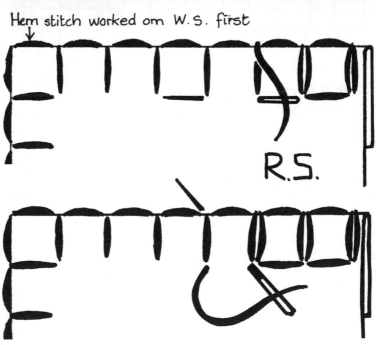

Hem stitch worked om W.S. first

R.S.

Trim off any surplus material on the wrong side close to the stitching.

Decorated picot edge

Work picot edge 3, trim material and then work three close rows of four-sided stitch. Leave about 3 threads and work a line of satin stitch. Leave another 3 threads and work two rows of honeycomb stitch.

This edging is sufficiently rich to form the main decoration of an item such as a small cloth or mat.

Fringed edging

Work two rows of three-sided stitch the required distance from the edge and fringe material away only when stitching is complete. This edging is not suitable for frequent laundering.

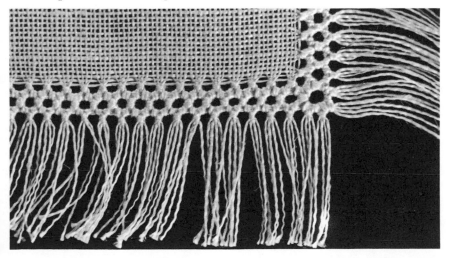

PULLED WORK IN THE PAST

In the comparatively short time available for preparation of a book of this sort it was only possible to see a limited selection of extant examples of pulled work, mainly in England, and therefore this chapter is not intended as a comprehensive survey of historical pulled work but rather as a guide to the reader to show how some embroiderers in the past have interpreted this method in ways which were influenced by their environment, the materials available to them, and contemporary fashions in clothes and furnishings.

In sketches, photographs and descriptions it is only possible to give an overall impression of any one piece, and it is far more valuable to go to a museum to see actual examples to truly appreciate the work of any one period, or even to assess why you dislike it. If the period sought is not on show, do not hesitate to ask if the museum has examples in its collections, as it may be possible to view pieces not on public display by arrangement with the museum authorities, who are usually extremely helpful.

Pulled work was often used on practical articles of dress and household linen. Many must have been lost in the inevitable process of wear and tear, laundering and decay, and sections or fragments of some pieces are now all that remain and it is only possible to guess at their original size and purpose. Purposes change too, and an article that was fairly commonplace two centuries ago may now extend our imaginations in trying to guess its original function; the success of television programmes where experts endeavour to place and date antiques confirms this difficulty in all fields of art and craft work. Textiles are also easily portable, so that their present resting place may be hundreds of miles away from their place of origin, and to fix a precise date and place of origin is work of detection and assumption. But looking at historical pieces of pulled work is extremely informative and at times quite stimulating when it is realised what a variety of ideas have been expressed in embroidery in the past; and as embroiderers of the second half of the twentieth century it is humbling to find that we do not have an exclusive claim to inventive and imaginative work, but that in the past our predecessors were equally willing to experiment with stitches, fabrics and a combination of techniques. It would appear that only in the early part of this century were strictures laid down on the 'correct' pulled thread technique, which led to much work of an extremely high technical standard but in many cases combined with stultified design: an approach that has not yet disappeared.

Unlike blackwork, pulled work does not have any distinctive style or period but tends to have a chameleon quality depending on which style of design and technique it is linked to, and the earliest pulled stitches may be just a few stitches worked more tightly than their fellows, as may be seen in odd rows of four-sided stitch on seventeenth-century samplers, for example. Mrs. Jackson shows 'Saracenic drawn linen' of about the eleventh century and a German example of the fourteenth century in *History of Lace*, but these are barely more than inventive weaving and the most obvious extant examples of early pulled thread work are Italian of the seventeenth century. These consist of bands where the background is worked in a pulled two-sided Italian cross stitch in colour, leaving the motif plain in the manner of Assisi work. The thread used is invariably silk on a fine or medium-weight linen and the designs vary from well-balanced geometric trees, animals and figures to motifs thrown willy-nilly on to the area of the band regardless of scale or balance, but often amusing and gay in their naïveté. The colour of thread is always rich: deep red, dark rose and dark green are common examples, and the stitching is completely regular, covering the whole background; only a little back stitch is used for detail on the motifs and occasionally as an outline. The stitching is not worked entirely in one direction, as both vertical and horizontal rows are worked, depending on the shape of the area to be filled. There are examples where double faggot stitch forms the background in similar designs. The original purpose of these bands and borders appears to have been lost because they have obviously been part of larger items, possibly for church linen, as an altar cover exists with a similar border but in another method of embroidery.

It is interesting that two-sided Italian cross stitch was then pulled very tightly, whereas now we consider it a canvas-work stitch, which suggests that other counted thread stitches could readily be interchangeable, simply by regulating the tension.

Another surprising form of pulled thread dating from the seventeenth or eighteenth century is shown in examples in the Benaki Museum in Athens; they at first appear to be lacis but on closer inspection show single or double faggot stitch used as a background on fairly fine linen on which some of the ground threads may have been removed to give a more open effect. Large panels and smaller items have been worked in this way and are further enriched either by darning with thick thread into the remaining material or by embroidering the motifs left in material with cross and chain stitches in colour.

During the eighteenth century in Western Europe, that is, in France, Germany, Denmark, Britain and the Low Countries, pulled thread truly became a technique in its own right. Although it plainly began as an imitation of lace it flowered into an original technique requiring a great deal of expertise. Lace-making is constructing a complete fabric from interwoven, knotted or needleworked threads, whereas pulled work began with a fine material which had its texture changed with stitchery. Its origins must also have been fostered by the fact that fine materials were readily available and became an important part of fashion. Some of these materials have names which we still use, cambric meaning a fine French linen, and lawn, which was also a fine linen, but others have quite unfamiliar names; jaconet, a slight soft muslin; nainsook, a Bengal muslin; sleasey, a flimsy silesian lawn and also selesie lawn, meaning a cambric from Silesia. In 1795 'cambric for ruffles' was 10s a yard and a man's handkerchief was 12s, both presumably embroidered at that price, and in 1795 'real India muslins' were from 6d to £1 16s per yard. From these delicate materials a variety of articles were made such as decorative aprons, fichus (then called handkerchiefs) and sleeve falls of which there are many extant examples.

Surprisingly it is very difficult to find examples of babies' clothes in pulled thread of this time, although there are many of Ayrshire embroidery which evolved from pulled thread, so that it can only be concluded that either they were made but due to wear and tear have been lost, or that the delicate materials were not considered suitable for babies' clothes in those days.

There is a baby's bonnet of the mid-eighteenth century in the Bath Museum of Costume, made of fine linen and embroidered in Italian quilting and trapunto with one layer cut away in places to allow a few pulled thread fillings; although charming to look at, the bumpy surfaces must have made it singularly uncomfortable for the baby to wear. The same museum has on show both men's and women's clothes worked with pulled thread, and one or two unusual pieces like a judge's 'lace' cuffs of 1730 which are beautifully worked, and a man's handkerchief which suggest that pulled thread was widely used in the eighteenth century.

During this century richly embroidered clothes for men were fashionable, mainly waistcoats and top coats, and there are quite a number of white twill waistcoats extant combining quilting, rich surface stitchery and pulled thread. It would appear that the quilting was worked first and then the twill was cut away in places so that the pulled thread fillings could be worked on the layer of backing linen. On one or two waistcoats it seems that the fillings are actually worked successfully on twill, which is about the most unsuitable material for the method. Hand-embroidered buttons were requisite to complete these handsome garments; the buttons were made over wooden moulds and, incidentally, if trimmed with french knots were called 'snails', but most unfairly the wearing of covered buttons was made illegal by Acts of both Anne and George I – probably fines were a good source of income from such a popular fashion!

Now to consider the items of dress in detail. Fichus, then called 'handkerchiefs', were of a triangular shape with the point at centre back and the two ends tucked under the front lacing on the bodice, making a soft frame for neck and face and covering the décolletage, and were not 'dress wear'. In *The Guardian* of 1713 a gentleman avers that 'when she [his wife] is at home she is continually muffled up and concealed in mobs [mob caps], morning gowns and handkerchiefs, but strips every afternoon to appear in public'. Perhaps this explains the dearth of portraits of this period illustrating pulled work fichus or sleeve falls; people would want to be painted in their best clothes to which there would have been real lace trimmings, and their Dresden or Tonder worked muslins would perhaps have been considered less impressive.

Tonder in Denmark produced a range of laces from as early as 1647 but was particularly noted for 'Tonder work' during the eighteenth century, which consists of extremely fine pulled thread fillings contained in elaborate floral designs worked on lawn or cambric. 'Dresden work' was in a similar style and both the Whitworth Art Gallery in Manchester and the Victoria and Albert Museum in London have superb German samplers of this time, the Manchester one being described as having been 'worked in a Rhenish nunnery'. Both are divided into many squares and in the London sampler the worker shows an incredible number of different fillings, worked so finely that it is necessary to look at them under a magnifying glass to fully appreciate their expertise and virtuosity, in a combination of stitchery and fabric exhibiting a wide selection of delicate textures. Evidently the fame of Dresden work was far spread, as there is a reference to being taught Dresden work in Anna Winslow's *Diary of a Boston Schoolgirl* of 1773; *American Needlework* mentions French émigrés who '. . . found solace and sometimes sustenance in teaching the fine art of white work they had learned in their youth' and in the same book there is an illustration of a white embroidered mull handkerchief of 1824 which undoubtedly contains skilful pulled work.

The points of the eighteenth-century fichus were usually richly embroidered with pulled fillings, as were the shorter edges of the triangle, although some have only edgings; sleeve falls, which could be in one, two or three gathered layers of fabric, were also embroidered with edgings of varying widths and were cut shorter on the inside of the elbow than on the outside so that in wear they fell in graceful folds revealing both sides of the embroidery.

Aprons were in fashion throughout the century, and were often embroidered in coloured silks or made of rich materials, but muslin or lawn aprons were also popular though fashion decreed that they were longer than other aprons, reaching almost to the ankle, and were purely decorative. There are examples of aprons richly embroidered with pulled work, but more often the work is slight with tamboured outlines of chain stitch enclosing only a few small areas of the simpler pulled thread fillings, such as single faggot, and rarely contain any of the skill and inventiveness shown on the more elaborately worked fichus. In the Folk Museum in Athens a square scarf of muslin on a national costume is designed and worked in an almost identical way to the aprons, but the link is too tenuous for us to be able to draw any conclusion.

The embroiderers of the eighteenth century, more often professional than amateur, intuitively understood the relationship of textures by contrasting smooth outlines of satin stitch, a flat wide buttonhole stitch or chain stitch with the broken textures of fillings, and thereby achieved a harmonious balance; shadow work was sometimes combined with pulled thread fillings as a more subtle textural contrast. The thread used for pulled thread fillings was fine and twisted, and some thread is incredibly fine considering that the methods of spinning were primitive compared with the mechanisation of this century, when paradoxically it is increasingly difficult to obtain strong, fine embroidery thread.

Pulled work on men's twill waistcoats was in quite a contrasting style to the fine work of ladies' clothes, being bold and balanced against quilting and surface stitchery worked in thickish thread; the effect is of shading using depth of texture rather than colour. A bold stylised floral design from shoulder to hem either side of the front opening would be thickly worked, using a range of thread thickness, some of the thread being glossy and some matt. There are unusual combinations of techniques, varying slightly from garment to garment, and pulled work fillings can be seen with surface stitches such as French knots and laid fillings, quilting (both English and trapunto) and round eyelets. Although the majority of articles showing this flamboyant mixture are waistcoats, in the Victoria and Albert Museum they have examples of a stomacher and underskirt and at Gawthorpe Hall an unfinished coverlet.

As embroiderers we have had a tendency to keep embroidery techniques strictly separated, but the modern argument for integrating a variety of methods experimentally is here seen illustrated by our predecessors as visually acceptable, and is found to be valid for practical articles and not only decorative items.

Gradually fashion advanced and other garments came into vogue, changing the style of decoration so that pulled fillings became less and less used while satin stitch was emphasised and eventually broderie Anglaise evolved at the beginning of the nineteenth century.

The eighteenth century has provided us with many examples of Western European dress where pulled work appears in consistent styles, but during the nineteenth and early twentieth centuries it resumes its chameleon quality and there are examples from such countries as Russia, India, Greece, Czechoslovakia, Spain, Turkey, Sicily and South America, showing mainly a use of the simpler fillings combined with other techniques. There are particularly interesting examples from Russia and the Greek Islands where single or double faggot stitch is worked as a bold background on coarse linen, leaving the design in plain material; the designs are simple and naïve in peasant tradition, but because of their vigour and straightforward approach are extremely effective. The articles made are invariably household linen, of which a buffet cloth is illustrated, and are sturdily made with a view to hard wear.

Nowadays Scandinavian countries are well known for their peasant tradition of attractive counted thread work, which includes much pulled thread and is successful in both geometric and figurative design simply because it is unpretentious and based on an inborn appreciation of scale and texture in combining stitches, thread and fabric. There is little point in trying to emulate the peasant tradition if we have been brought up in the sophisticated industrial environment of modern countries, but we can try to embroider with their honesty of approach. Historical work teaches us that each age has been unconsciously influenced by trends in fashion and décor, by trade and wars affecting the availability of threads and materials and by other apparently extraneous influences. Embroidery should reflect the age in which it is worked in the same way as art, fashion, furniture and other crafts; experiment is essential to counteract a stagnation of ideas and must needs result in some work of a high aesthetic value.

179

Italian seventeenth century. This angel forms the basis
of the repetitive border together with an exotic bird
and plant motif and the initials N.I. The background
of the border, which is about 4″ (10 cm) wide, is in
two-sided Italian cross stitch. (By kind permission of
the Victoria and Albert Museum.)

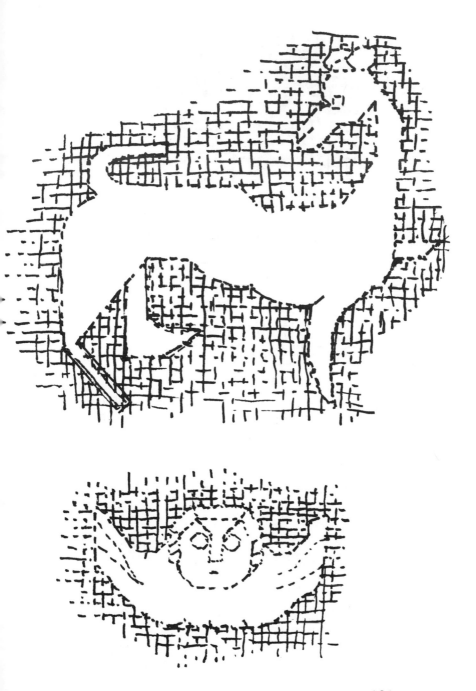

181

Three motifs from a border about 6″ (15 cm) wide
where animals, snakes, griffons and cherubs are shown
arranged haphazardly in a repeated design. The
background is in fine two-sided Italian cross stitch in
deep rose-pink silk thread. (By kind permission of the
Victoria and Albert Museum.)

Opposite:
Italian seventeenth century. A crisply designed oak
tree forms the motif for a repeating vertical border.
The background and outlines within the design are
two-sided Italian cross stitch in strawberry-pink twisted
silk on white linen. The designer has shown
understanding of the technique as the stitches fit easily
into the stylised shapes. (By kind permission of the
Whitworth Art Gallery, University of Manchester.)

182

Italian seventeenth century. A competent, professional-
looking border, heraldic in style. The design has
obviously been made specifically for this width of
border. Rust-red two-sided Italian cross stitch forms
the background. (By kind permission of the Victoria
and Albert Museum.)

Overleaf left:
Leucas, Ionian Islands. Seventeenth/eighteenth
century. This is a colourful, richly embroidered
hanging although the motifs themselves are primitive
in design. The background is in single faggot stitch and
the figures are embroidered in red, green, and orange
in cross and chain stitches. (By kind permission of the
Benaki Museum, Athens.)

184

Overleaf right:
At first sight it would seem likely·that this panel had
come from Scandinavia rather than the Dodecanese by
the style of design, in its fresh simplicity and
understanding of designing within the limitations of the
counted thread technique. Some threads were probably
removed before working the background in double
faggot stitch to give a more open effect, and then a
thickish thread was used to emphasise the motifs with
darning or double running stitch. The face shows how,
with a minimum of detail, features, character and
expression can be suggested. Seventeenth or eighteenth
century. (By kind permission of the Benaki Museum,
Athens.)

Silk
brocade
dress.

cap.

fichu (handkerchief)
shallow point at
back.

Sleeve fall

Apron

This is a sketch to show articles of dress that were
embroidered with pulled work as they would have
appeared in wear, about the middle of the eighteenth
century in England.

188

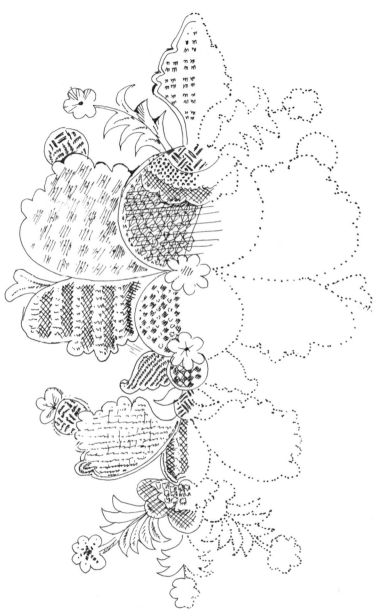

This drawing is of an elaborate motif worked in the point of a fichu and containing a wide variety of fillings, outlined with chain stitch and buttonhole

stitch. It dates from the first half of the eighteenth
century. (By kind permission of the City of Liverpool
Museum.)

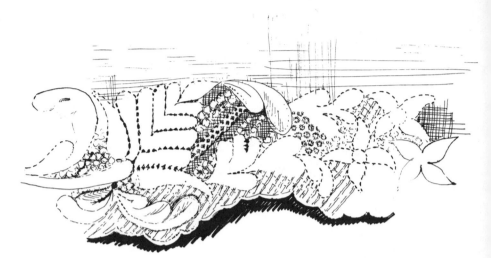

Border from the edge of a fichu very finely
embroidered in shadow work and pulled thread fillings,
about actual size. (By kind permission of the City of
Liverpool Museum.)

Opposite:
Basic floral design from a sleeve fall with an elaborate
scalloped edge; the outlines are either button-holed or
chain-stitched and enclose a variety of fillings.
Eighteenth century. (By kind permission of Liverpool
City Museum.)

190

Basic design from the corner of a muslin apron worked
mainly in chain stitch as the design, although pretty,
provides for only small areas of pulled fillings in the
floral shapes and scalloped edge. Eighteenth century.
(By kind permission of the City of Liverpool Museum.)

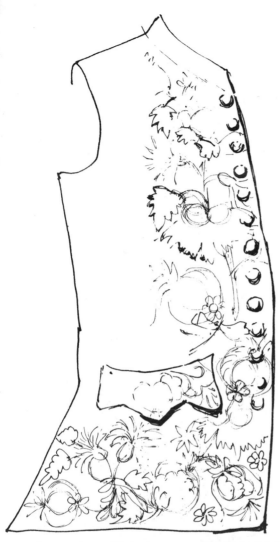

Gentleman's twill waistcoat of 1760–70 lined with
linen; the whole design is richly embroidered in
off-white in a mixture of techniques, including pulled
work. The pocket flap is purely decorative and it is
quite possible that some of the buttons, embroidered
with a satin stitch star, were never intended to enter
the many buttonholes. (By kind permission of the City
of Liverpool Museum.)

Opposite:
Part of the basic design of the embroidery on the
preceding waistcoat showing the bold floral shapes
based on carnations, pomegranates and forget-me-nots.

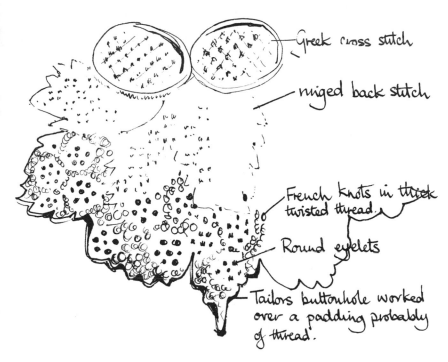

Greek cross stitch

ruged back stitch

French knots in thick
twisted thread.

Round eyelets

Tailors buttonhole worked
over a padding probably
of thread.

Detail showing the stitches used to give an effect of
shading with depth of texture rather than colour, on
the preceding waistcoat.

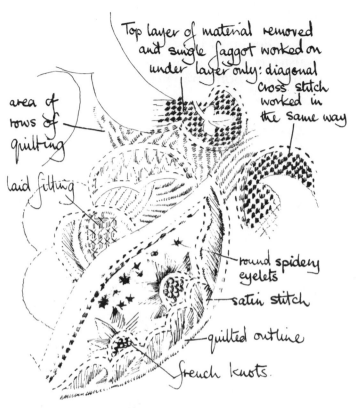

Part of an unfinished coverlet combining a variety of
techniques. (By kind permission of the trustees of
Gawthorpe Hall.)

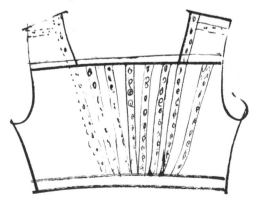

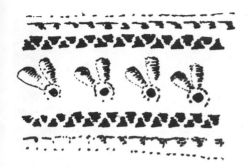

Opposite below:
Sketch of an Empire chemisette at Gawthorpe Hall
which is skilfully shaped by inserting bands of
embroidery between crossway cut sections. The above
insertion shows satin stitch, round eyelets, single rows
of honeycomb stitch and a pulled back stitch, and
demonstrates in a small way the transition between
the pulled work of the eighteenth century and broderie
Anglaise.

Overleaf:
Russian early nineteenth century. This is the wide
border of a buffet cloth of formal motifs outlined very
boldly in two rows of chain stitch in a thick thread,
giving an almost sculptured appearance against the
background of single faggot. The round eyelets are
rather inexpertly executed, but the whole piece has
great vigour and is on a suitably bold scale for a large
cloth which might well have been viewed across a large
room. (By kind permission of the Whitworth Art
Gallery, University of Manchester.)

197

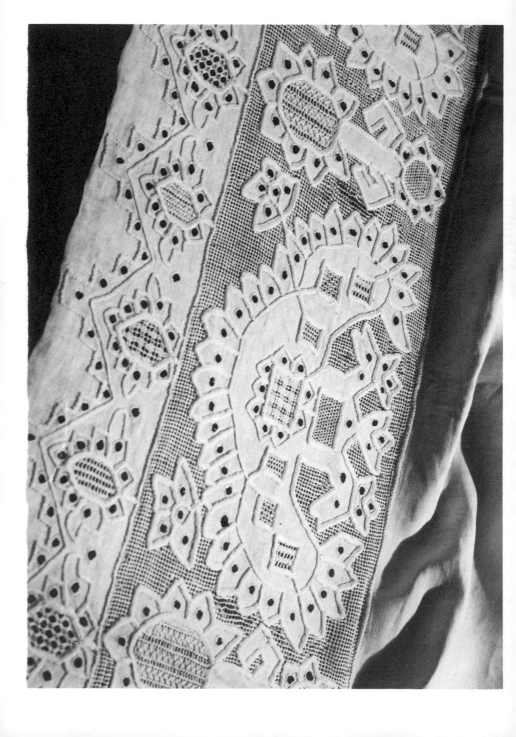

Another wide band forming a frieze of animal, ship and human motifs in a strong peasant tradition. The background is worked in double faggot stitch on a coarse cotton ground and the whole is described as a bed edge. (Greek, probably this century, in the Wace Collection at Liverpool City Museum.)

Overleaf left:
Part of a German eighteenth-century sampler illustrating the skill and inventiveness of the worker. (By courtesy of the Victoria and Albert Museum.)

Overleaf right:
A mat worked in Germany in 1937 shows the same high standard of technical skill as in the eighteenth century. (The Needlework Development Scheme collection at the Embroiderers' Guild.)

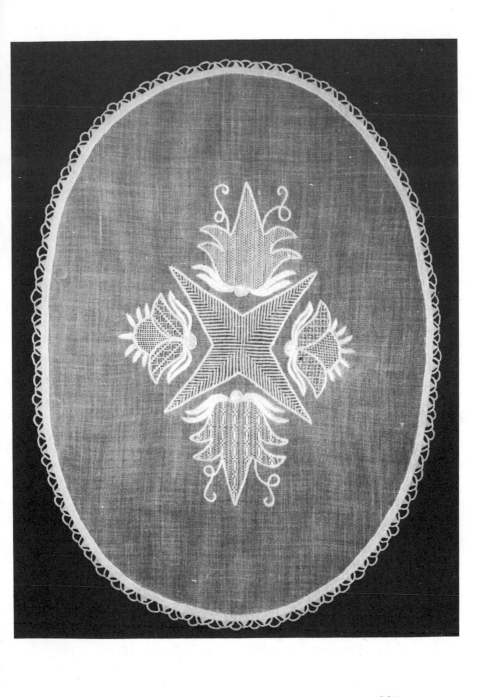

Part of the front panel from an unfinished christening robe of the nineteenth century. The figures, mainly in French knots and trailing, stand out against a background of single faggot stitch. (The Needlework Development Scheme collection at the Embroiderers' Guild.)

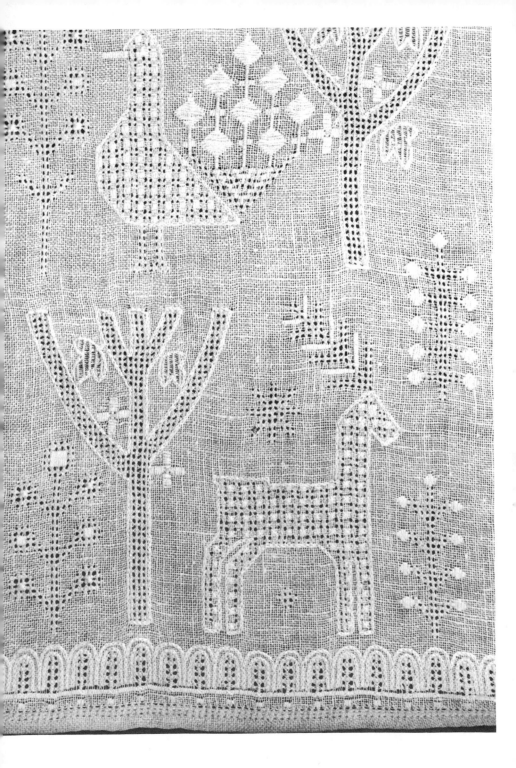

Previous page:
An attractive Swedish cloth of 1947 shows simply
shaped and worked motifs on a thick, rich linen.
Four-sided stitch and satin stitch with chain-stitch
outlining are the main stitches used. (The Needlework
Development Scheme collection at the Embroiderers'
Guild.)

Overleaf:
A deceptively simple design on a Norwegian mat of
1949, based on the change of stitch direction. Astrid
Sandvold. (The Needlework Development Scheme
collection at the Embroiderers' Guild.)

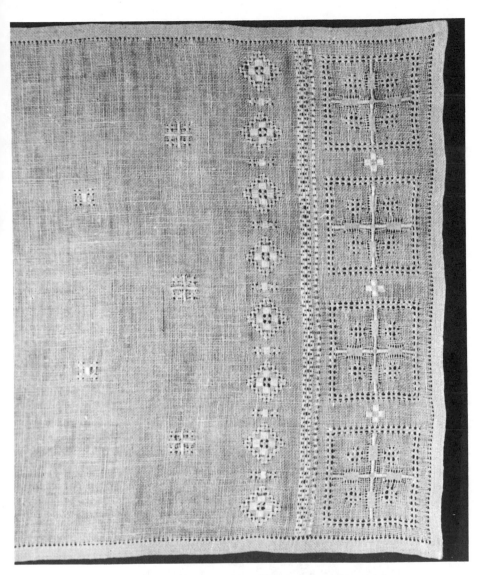

Worked on a grey linen mat is an effective border with spot motifs to decorate the centre; note how the spots are varied to avoid tedium. Svensk Hemslojd, 1948, Sweden. (The Needlework Development Scheme collection at the Embroiderers' Guild.)